I0493015

CEO Guide to Doing Business in South Korea

By Ade Asefeso MCIPS MBA

Second Edition

ISBN-13: 978-1500100964

ISBN-10: 150010096X

Publisher: AA Global Sourcing Ltd
Website: http://www.aaglobalsourcing.com

Table of Contents

Disclaimer

This publication is designed to provide competent and reliable information regarding the subject matter covered. However, it is sold with the understanding that the author and publisher are not engaged in rendering professional advice. The authors and publishers specifically disclaim any liability that is incurred from the use or application of contents of this book.

If you purchased this book without a cover you should be aware that this book may have been stolen property and reported as "unsold and destroyed" to the publisher. In this case neither the author nor the publisher has received any payment for this "stripped book."

Dedication

This book is dedicated to the hundreds of thousands of incredible souls in the world who have weathered through the up and down of recent recession.

To my family and friends who seems to have been sent here to teach me something about who I am supposed to be. They have nurtured me, challenged me, and even opposed me.... But at every juncture has taught me!

This book is dedicated to my lovely boys, Thomas, Michael and Karl. Teaching them to manage their finance will give them the lives they deserve. They have taught me more about life, presence, and energy management than anything I have done in my life.

Chapter 1: Introduction

Over the past four decades, South Korea's impressive economic growth was part of what has been described as the "East Asian miracle." Intensive growth transformed South Korea into the 12th largest economy and trading partner in the world in 2006. It was driven by high savings rates and investment and a strong emphasis on education, which boosted the number of young people enrolled in a college or university to one of the highest levels in the world (82.1% in 2005).

During those years, South Korea's industrial structure was drastically reshaped. Major industries were diversified to include automobiles, petrochemicals, electronics, shipbuilding, textiles and steel products. By applying lessons from centuries of development in the West, South Korea was able to make a similar transformation from an agricultural to manufacturing and on to a service-cantered economy in just 50. Thanks to the GDP growth driven by brisk export and sizeable investment in plant and facilities. South Korea emerged as the world's 11th largest economy in terms of GDP, which reached US$887.4 billion in 2006.

South Korea is now a high-tech economy. It is a world leader in electronics manufacturing, including semiconductor chips, flat-screen TVs and mobile phones. Samsung the world's largest electronics company originated in South Korea. The organisation has a turnover greater than that of Apple, Google and Microsoft combined.

South Korea also has the highest level of broadband penetration in the world (with speeds of 100 megabytes), as well as the highest 3G mobile usage. Moreover, the country is a world leader in shipbuilding, steel and automotive. Its construction and energy companies are increasingly successful overseas.

The population is highly educated. Seven per cent of the country's entire GDP is spent on education and nearly three quarters (74 per cent) of South Koreans undertake postgraduate-level study. This creates excellent opportunities for foreign educational institutions.

In July 2011, the EU-South Korea Free Trade Agreement (FTA) came into force. The historic agreement presents opportunities for greater EU-Korean collaboration; based on current trading patterns it will be worth at least £500 million per annum to the UK economy. The most comprehensive FTA ever agreed between two parties, the deal will create outstanding opportunities in financial services, telecommunications and legal services. Ninety seven per cent of tariff barriers between Korea and the EU will be eliminated within three years and €1.6 billion of duties for EU exporters will be abolished annually.

South Korea is the world's 12th-largest economy. It has a GDP of over US$1 trillion just less than the size of the entire Association of Southeast Asian Nations (ASEAN) and equal to 2 per cent of global GDP. Per capita purchasing power is some US$30,000.

Inward investment: Many South Korean companies have chosen to invest in the UK. There are currently around 170 South Korean firms doing business in Britain, with the largest investors being Doosan (which owns Doosan Babcock HQ in Scotland and has offices across the UK), Samsung and LG Electronics (both of whom have their European headquarters and design/R&D facilities in the UK).

The Korea National Pension Service, while not yet physically present in the UK, has spent over US$1 billion on infrastructure assets in the country, including the HSBC Tower in London's Canary Wharf and a 12 per cent stake in Gatwick Airport.

According to the South Korean government, the UK was the largest foreign direct investor in South Korea in 2009, investing US$1.9 billion. In fact, over the last 45 years, the UK has been the second-largest EU investor in South Korea, in cumulative terms. Tesco and Standard Chartered are among the country's largest foreign investors, investing between £2-3 billion each.

Chapter 2: South Korea at a Glance

Full name: The Republic of Korea

Capital: Seoul

Other main cities: Busan, Incheon, Daegu

Area: 99,313 sq. km (38,345 sq. miles)

Population: 48.2 million (2010), one million foreign residents

Major languages: Korean (written form Hangul) English is widely spoken

Ethnicities: Korean, with the exception of around 20,000 Chinese

Life expectancy: 76 years (men), 83 years (women)

Major religions: Buddhism, Christianity

Monetary unit: South Korean won (KRW)

Nominal GDP: US$986.3 billion (2010)

GDP per capita: US$31,700 (2011)

World Bank ease of doing business ranking: 8 (2011)

Over the next five years, the South Korean economy is set to make the 10th-largest contribution to world growth. That is as much as the UK and more than France or Italy. Despite the global slowdown, South Korea's economy grew by 3.6 per cent in 2011, the fastest in the OECD (Organisation for Economic Co-operation and Development).

Geography

The Korean Peninsula, which lies on the north-eastern edge of the Asian continent shares its northern border with China and Russia and juts toward Japan to the southeast. Korea is roughly 1,000 kilometres long and encompasses a total of 222,154 square kilometres (South Korea - 99,392 sq. km; North Korea - 122,762 sq. km). It is nearly the same size as Britain and a little larger than Portugal. The Republic of Korea is populated by 48.6 million people as of 2008.

Climate

The Korean Peninsula, which is situated at the eastern edge of the Eurasian continent, lies between and north latitude. With the Taebaek mountain range forming the backbone of the Korean Peninsula, Korea has a diverse climate in spite of its small size. It lies in the temperate zone, and has four distinct seasons as well as diverse topography. The transitional seasons, spring and autumn, are generally sunny and clear, although they are short in comparison to winter and summer and have distinct weather patterns.

Language and Currency

In 1443, King Sejong promoted the creation of an alphabet for writing that could simply and accurately convey the sounds of the spoken language. Originally known as Hunminjeongeum, or "the correct sounds for the instruction of the people," it is an easy-to-learn phonetic alphabet that enabled the common people to express themselves in writing. Hangeul, as the alphabet has come to be known, is unique among the world's writing systems as its creation is well documented, including the date it originated and the names of the people who invented it. The unit of Korean currency is the Won (indicated as).

Legal System

The South Korean legal system effectively dates from the introduction of the original Constitution of the Republic of Korea and the organization of South Korea as an independent state. During the existence of the Republic of Korea, the Constitution has been revised or rewritten several times, the most recent of which was in 1987 at the beginning of the Sixth Republic.

The Court Organization Act, which was passed into law on 26 September 1949, officially created a three-tiered, independent judicial system in the Republic of Korea.

The revised Constitution of 1987 guaranteed that judges would not be removed from office for any reason other than impeachment, criminal acts, or incapacity. Additionally, the 1987 Constitution officially codified judicial independence in Article 103, which states that, "Judges rule independently according to their conscience and in conformity with the Constitution and the law." In addition to the new guarantees of judicial independence, the 1987 rewrite of the Constitution established the Constitutional Court, marking the first time that South Korea had an active body for constitutional review.

The judicial system of South Korea is composed of the Supreme Court of South Korea, the Constitutional Court of South Korea, six High Courts, 13 District Courts, and several courts of specialized jurisdiction, such as the Family Court and Administrative Court. In addition, branches of District Courts may be established, as well as Municipal Courts. South Korean courts are organized and empowered in chapters V and VI of the Constitution of the Republic of Korea.

There is no system of juries in the judicial system of South Korea, although since Feb 2nd 2008 a limited system of juries has been adopted for criminal cases and environmental cases, and all questions of law and fact are decided by judges.

Advantages of Investing in Korea

The Republic of Korea is located between China and Japan. Its geopolitical position has enabled Korea to act as a bridge for cultural exchanges and trade between its neighbours. In this regard, Korea is an optimal location for doing business with China (the largest market in the world), and Japan (the world's 2nd biggest economy).

North Asia is home to 25% of the world's population and generates 22% of its GDP (forecasted to increase to 30% by 2020).

Korea has rapidly emerged as one of the world's leading ICT (Information and Communication Technology) powerhouses. Korea's excellent telecommunications infrastructure makes Internet use and maintenance easily affordable. Its outstanding edge and competitiveness enabled Seoul to rank top in the UN Global e-Government Survey. Korea's e-Government program was exported to Moscow, Russia in 2004, and Hanoi, Vietnam in 2005.

Korea is the world's 8th largest investor in research and development (IMD 2003). Annual R&D investment has increased steadily since 1997, well above the rate of GDP growth. Although R&D investment temporarily shrunk in 1999 because of the economic slowdown caused by the Asian financial crisis, it has been on the rebound since 1999.

The R&D investment in 2005 stood at US$ 24.1 billion, or 2.99% of GDP, which is close to the highest level in the world. Korea's responsiveness to the latest products and services make the country an ideal test bend. In fact, a number of global companies take advantage of this responsiveness to utilize Korea's leading infrastructure and dynamic market.

Constitution

The Republic of Korea (commonly known as "South Korea") is a republic with powers nominally shared among the presidency, the legislature, and the judiciary, but traditionally dominated by the president. The president is chief of state and is elected for a single term of 5 years. The 299 members of the unicameral National Assembly are elected to 4-year terms; elections for the assembly were held on April 9, 2008.

South Korea's judicial system comprises a Supreme Court, appellate courts, and a Constitutional Court. The judiciary is independent under the constitution. The country has nine provinces and seven administratively separate cities; the capital of Seoul, along with Busan, Daegu, Daejeon, Gwangju, Incheon and Ulsan.

Chapter 3: Opportunities in South Korea for Foreign Companies

We designated South Korea as a high growth market and identified significant opportunities in the following sectors:

Aerospace – The South Korean government is looking to develop a small and medium-sized aircraft manufacturing value chain, led by its single aircraft manufacturer, Korean Airspace Industries Ltd. There are opportunities for foreign companies to supply and collaborate.

Creative industries (Design) – South Korea's overall design market is worth £10.6 billion. Seoul was the World Design Capital in 2010 and encouraged new and creative design concepts in and around the city. UK design is highly valued by Korean companies.

ICT (Communications, Industrial Electronics, Consumer Electronics) – South Korea leads the world in many applications, including digital media broadcasting (DMB). There are many opportunities for UK companies involved in areas such as embedded software; 4G mobile telephony; games (including mobile games); bio-recognition systems and internet security; and green ICT.

In addition to these strategic priority sectors, there are also many other commercial opportunities for foreign companies in the following areas:

Automotive – South Korea has been the world's fifth-largest automotive producer for three consecutive years and offers wide-ranging opportunities for auto supply, component and design companies, particularly in the development of low carbon and electric vehicles.

Consumer products – South Korea is a sophisticated market with steadily increasing levels of disposable income. Most major luxury brands are represented, with many rating South Korea as one of their most profitable markets. Major opportunities exist in fashion, and in food and drink.

Education – South Korea is one of the largest education markets in the world. English-language training, including training delivered via e-learning, offers considerable opportunities.

Energy – South Korea currently imports 96 per cent of its primary energy needs, but is seeking to reduce significantly its dependency on oil and gas imports by generating power from renewable sources. Opportunities exist in wind, wave, solar and CCS (Carbon Capture & Storage), in R&D and full commercial-scale projects.

Environment – President Lee Myung-bak's "Green Growth" policies are creating multiple opportunities in the development and application of green technologies, particularly in reducing carbon emissions from industry and buildings. There are also niche opportunities in water and waste management, and in air pollution abatement.

Financial and legal services – The EU-South Korea FTA will remove some key barriers to the profitability of UK banks in the country and, gradually, allow UK law firms access to the South Korean market. There are particular opportunities for asset management companies to work alongside Korean sovereign wealth funds, including the Korean National Pension Service (the fourth largest in the world), and the Korean Investment Corporation.

Life Sciences – South Korea's rapidly ageing population and societal drivers for a healthier lifestyle ensure a wide range of opportunities, from the supply of branded drugs to over-the-counter supplements, with natural ingredient based products in particularly high demand. South Korea is a developed market for healthcare provision, offering niche opportunities in the supply of high-end equipment and telemedicine.

Chapter 4: Choosing the Right Location

The Korean Peninsula lies in the north eastern part of the Asian continent. It is bordered to the north by Russia and China, to the east by the East Sea and Japan, and to the west by the Yellow Sea. In addition to the mainland, South Korea comprises around 3,200 islands, including Jejudo, Ulleungdo and Dokdo.

At 99,313 sq. km, the country is slightly larger than Austria. It has one of the highest population densities in the world, after Bangladesh and Taiwan, with more than 50 per cent of its population living in the country's six largest cities.

Korea has a history spanning 5,000 years and you will find evidence of its rich and varied heritage in the many temples, palaces and city gates. These sit alongside contemporary architecture that reflects the growing economic importance of South Korea as an industrialised nation.

In 1948, Korea divided into North Korea and South Korea. North Korea was allied to the, then, USSR and South Korea to the USA. The divide between the two countries at Panmunjom is one of the world's most heavily fortified frontiers. Surrounded on three sides by the ocean, it is easy to see how South Korea became a world leader in shipbuilding.

Climate

South Korea has a temperate climate, with four distinct seasons. Spring, from late March to May, is warm, while summer, from June to early September is hot and humid. Autumn, from late September to November, is generally mild. Winters in Korea tend to be bitterly cold, due to Siberian airflows, and there can be heavy snow in northern and eastern parts.

Centres of business

Seoul – is the capital of South Korea and its largest commercial centre. With a population of around 10 million, it is one of the largest cities in the world. The Seoul National Capital Area, which is generally referred to as Sudogwon, is the second largest metropolitan area in the world. It has over 24.5 million inhabitants and includes the Incheon metropolis and most of Gyeonggi province.

There are a range of industrial clusters outside Seoul, including:

Osong Bio-Technopolis – South Korea's first bio cluster, located 170km south of Seoul. Osong is designated a special zone for foreign direct investment, securing US$260 million to date. Foreign companies seeking to invest in the complex will be exempt from rent and corporate taxes for five to seven years, with additional tax benefits offered by the local government.

South East Coast and Ulsan – is where South Korea's world-leading shipbuilding cluster is located. The cluster is home to manufacturers of steel plates, steel structures and engines, as well as colleges specialising in shipbuilding and marine engineering. Ulsan shipyard is currently the largest in the world and has the capacity to build a variety of vessels, including commercial cargo, offshore and naval.

Busan (officially Busan Metropolitan City and formerly spelled Pusan) – is the second-largest metropolis in South Korea after Seoul. It is the largest port city in the country and the fifth-largest port in the world. Busan has played host to several high-profile international business and sporting events, including the APEC Economic Leaders Meeting in 2005. The largest department store in the world, Shinsegae Centum City, is located there and Busan is building many super-skyscrapers, including the 110-floor Lotte Super Tower.

Incheon (officially Incheon Metropolitan City) – is part of the Seoul National Capital Area and is the third-largest urban area in South Korea, behind Seoul and Busan. Incheon is the country's most important transport hub, housing the largest seaport on the west coast and the country's largest airport. Global business is centred around the high-tech Songdo International City, which is the site of South Korea's tallest building, the Northeast Asia Trade Tower.

Incheon was South Korea's first Free Economic Zone, providing various types of government services to promote foreign investment. For example, English is the official language for government documents in this area and, in September 2010, the Chadwick International School – the first in the region – opened in the Songdo district. Incheon's goal is to transform three of its districts (Songdo, Yeongjong and Cheongna) into the logistics, leisure and tourism, and international business hubs of the Northeast Asia region.

Incheon will play host to the Asian Games in 2014, from 19 September to 4 October. It beat off India to host the Games and is the third city in South Korea after Seoul (1986) and Busan (2002) to stage the event.

Daegu (officially the Daegu Metropolitan City) – is one of the largest metropolitan areas in South Korea, with more than 2.5 million people. The city is located in south eastern Korea, about 80km from the coast. It is a centre for fashion and high-tech industries.

Songdo – this district of Incheon is aiming to become a global city of high-tech knowledge and international business. The Samsung Group recently announced a US$266 million venture with partner Quintiles Transnational Corp. to make biologic drugs here. The new plant, which will contract-make medicines from living cells, will help Samsung to tap into South Korea's massive biopharmaceuticals market, which has produced five of the world's 10 best-selling medicines.

Yeongjong – is aiming to become an international logistics city. It is the site of Incheon International Airport and harbour. Expansion plans for the airport include creating a free trade zone, international business district and special economic zone. In March 2009, it was named Best Airport Worldwide in the Airport Service Quality Awards.

Cheongna – is aiming to become a global entertainment and tourist city, with several high-profile sports and leisure developments.

Other major centres in South Korea include: Suwon, Goyang, Seongnam and Bucheon.

Chapter 5: Market Entry via Agents and Distributors

An agent is a company's direct representative in a market and is paid commission, whereas a distributor buys products from the manufacturer and sells them on to customers. The difference between the cost of purchasing products and selling them on (the profit) forms the distributor's income. In South Korea, registered commissioned agents are known as "offer agents". Many of them operate on a small scale and lack capital, but if they have the right contacts they can provide adequate representation, even for major projects.

Entering a market by working with an agent or distributor can have several advantages. It reduces time and costs, and companies gain the local knowledge and networks of the agent/distributor in question. However, there are also some drawbacks. Employing a third party results in an additional cost to your products and you may lose some control and visibility over sales and marketing. It also has implications for intellectual property rights protection, increasing the risk of your product being copied or counterfeited. Given these considerations, you need to select agents and distributors carefully.

Suggested questions to ask agents/distributors are listed below.

You should also conduct due diligence to verify this information.

Background
1. Company size, history and ownership (private or state-owned).
2. Quality and quantity of the sales force.
3. Customer feedback and trade/bank references.

Distribution channels
1. Regional coverage.
2. Types of outlets covered and frequency of visits.
3. Transportation and warehousing facilities.

Are they right for you?
1. Does the agent/distributor have a genuine interest in representing your product?
2. Can they benefit from actively promoting your interests (is it a win-win)?
3. Do they also represent any competing companies or products?
4. Can you communicate effectively with your counterpart?

Once a working relationship has been established, the agent/distributor needs you to actively manage them by:
1. Visiting as regularly as is practicable at a senior management level. This shows interest in and commitment to, the agent and the market. It will also provide you with an

opportunity to learn about conditions in the market and see how your products are doing.

2. Working closely with the agent to show them how they can profit from your products.

3. Helping to prepare marketing and sales plans for the agent.

4. Providing regular training for sales staff and after-sales training for technical staff.

Chapter 6: Establishing a Presence in South Korea

Direct sales into South Korea can be difficult. For most foreign companies, it is more effective to approach the market through local business partners (agents and distributors) who have the ability to distribute and provide locally based technical support.

Licensing and franchising

Licensing and franchising are alternative approaches to selling products and services, but the exact business model will vary, depending on the sector and company. It is worth noting that Koreans have a different view of contractual agreements than UK companies. There is a tendency to regard them as "gentlemen's agreements" that can be subject to renegotiation if circumstances change, rather than as a binding contract. It is a good idea to exercise caution when entering into licensing agreements.

Having a permanent in-market presence can have several benefits, including:
1. Demonstrating commitment.
2. Cutting out the 'middle man', providing direct access to the end customer/supplier.
3. Giving direct control over corporate strategy and activities.
4. Enabling trading in the local currency and easing the conduct of business transactions

In the past, foreign investors who wanted to do business in South Korea were required to have a South Korean partner. However, this has changed, thanks to the South Korean government's continued efforts to ease regulations and encourage more foreign investors. It is now possible for foreign companies to establish a business in South Korea, even as sole traders, providing they follow the correct guidelines and procedures and set themselves up as an appropriate legal entity.

The company must also be compliant with South Korean legal and tax requirements. The South Korean government website contains information about how to set up a business in the country.

Once you have decided where you did like to establish your business, contact the local government office in your target region. These offices provide help for companies wishing to set up in their locality. There are details of metropolitan and provincial governments on the Korea.net website.

Deciding what constitutes an appropriate legal entity for your business depends on your intended scope. There are a number of legal structures that allow foreign invested enterprises (FIEs) to do business in South Korea, as outlined below. Each has its own advantages, restrictions and drawbacks, so it is essential to choose the option best suited to your aims.

It is usually more difficult to alter a business structure once a legal entity has been incorporated or established, so it is essential to seek professional advice during the early stages of planning.

Legal structures

Foreign invested enterprises (FIEs) in South Korea are governed by the Foreign Investment Promotion Act (FIPA) and the Commercial Code of Korea. The aim of FIPA is to create a level playing field between Korean investors and foreign investors, so that both are treated more or less equally. FIPA states that:

1. Foreign investors can invest in virtually any type of business in South Korea.
2. Potential foreign investors only have to notify the relevant government authorities, rather than having to seek consent.

FIEs established under FIPA are entitled to certain tax incentives provided by the Special Tax Treatment Control Act of Korea. In return, they are required to invest 50 million Korean won (approximately £28,000) or more in the local corporation. The Korean National Tax Service provides information about the taxation system for foreign investors.

Representative offices

Representative offices are often the first step taken by foreign companies when establishing a permanent presence in South Korea. They provide a vehicle through which the foreign investor can undertake activities such as market research, customer liaison and support. Representative offices can also organise business visits from company headquarters, which can make the process of obtaining business visas for visitors much easier. Public relations work and local administration are also permitted. However, a representative office cannot conduct sales activities. This means they cannot sign contracts; receive income or issue invoices and tax receipts.

Branch offices

Branch offices can be used for companies that do not plan to have their head office in South Korea but need the ability to exercise their rights, based on the South Korean legal system, and establish their own property there. A registration fee is payable, based on the authorised share capital of the parent company. A higher registration fee is payable if the parent company has a high authorised share capital.

Joint ventures

A joint venture (JV) is an organisation jointly owned by one or several South Korean and foreign partners. It can be formed by way of equity contribution, whereby ownership, risk and profit are shared, based on each party's monetary contribution.

Alternatively, a JV can be incorporated, with liabilities and profit distribution being decided by contractual agreement. JVs can be beneficial in a number of ways. A good local partner may contribute market knowledge and strong marketing and distribution channels, and they may help reduce the costs and risk of market entry.

The challenge of establishing and running a successful JV is to find and nurture the right partnership. Partners have to overcome issues such as mismatched expectations and differences in business culture and practices. The ability to maintain effective communication, and control, where necessary, is also crucial. It is essential that you carry out corporate and financial due diligence before you sign up to any partnership. Companies should also plan an exit strategy. Like a marriage, it is better to have a pre-nuptial agreement than a messy divorce.

Chapter 7: Foreign Investment Procedures in South Korea

Foreign investment procedures consists of submission of a foreign investment report, remittance of investment funds, registration of a foreign-invested company and registration of incorporation and business.

Where a foreign investor registers a privately-owned business, 'registration of incorporation' is not required. The procedures applied to foreigners are basically the same as for Koreans except for the two additional areas; foreign investment reports and registration of a foreign-invested company.

Foreign investment report

A foreign investor, or an agent, may report their investment at Invest KOREA (KOTRA), Korea Business Centres (KBC) of KOTRA, headquarters and branches of domestic foreign exchange banks, or domestic branches of delegated foreign banks.

1. **Reporting person:** A foreign investor or an agent.
2. **Delegated agency:** Headquarters and branches of domestic banks, domestic branches of delegated foreign banks, Invest KOREA (KOTRA), or Korea Business Centres (KBC) of KOTRA

3. **Processing period of a foreign investment report:** Immediate (The certificate of completion of report is issued without delay).

Follow-up management of foreign investment

Where a foreign investor or a foreign-invested company has completed payment for an investment or acquired existing stocks, he/she/it shall take procedures to register a foreign-invested company to the president of KOTRA or the Head of a foreign exchange bank, as prescribed by Acts and statutes of the Republic of Korea. The registration may be cancelled for certain reasons.

Corporation establishment

There are four ways that a foreign company can establish a business in South Korea:
1. A local corporation.
2. A private business set up by a foreigner or a foreign corporation (both recognised as a foreign investment).
3. A local branch.
4. A local office in South Korea set up by a foreign corporation.
5. (both categorised as a domestic branch of the foreign corporation).

Comparison of a foreign-invested company and a domestic branch

A foreign-invested company under the Foreign Investment Promotion Act Establishment of a local corporation in South Korea by a foreign national or a foreign corporation is regulated by the Foreign Investment Promotion Act and the Commercial Act. A foreigner shall invest not less than 100 million Korean Won for the local corporation concerned to be recognised as foreign investment under the Foreign Investment Promotion Act.

Private business established by a foreigner with the investment of not less than 100 million Korean Won, is also recognised as foreign investment under the Foreign Investment Promotion Act.

Domestic branch of a non-resident (a foreign company) under the Foreign Exchange Transactions Act A 'branch' that operates its business and generates profits in South Korea is not recognised as foreign direct investment.

An 'office' can be defined in that it does not carry out business that generates profits in South Korea, but instead undertakes a non-sales function such as market research, R&D etc. An 'office' is granted a distinct number (equivalent to business registration), at a jurisdictional tax office in South Korea without the need for registration, which is different from a 'branch.' For further details on incorporating in South Korea, contact or visit the offices of the Korean Trade Promotion Agency (KOTRA).

Chapter 8: Carry out your Due Diligence

The shareholders of the company are responsible for the amount of liability as stated as registered capital on the business licence. You can check whether or not the registered capital has been paid up by using a firm of accountants to get a Capital Verification Report.

If you want to establish a business relationship that goes beyond exporting, you will need to carry out further research. It is not enough simply to obtain a copy of a company's accounts, as they may not be accurate. Accounts in South Korea are unlikely to be audited to the standards routinely expected in the UK, and companies may have different sets of accounts for different audiences, so it is advisable to use such data in conjunction with information obtained from elsewhere.

Good-quality consultancy and assistance is available from firms resident in South Korea and the UK. These companies can carry out operational, financial, legal and technical due diligence checks, typically by looking at the actual operation of the business, and building up a more accurate picture by carefully interviewing people who work in and with the firm.

Many of the problems that foreign companies encounter when doing business in South Korea could have been avoided by carrying out some due diligence at the outset.

There are different levels of due diligence, appropriate for different situations. If your sole interest is in exporting, the best proof of a South Korean company's ability to pay is a letter of credit from the bank. If a company can produce this, you do not need to check its financial standing as the bank will have already done so.

A very simple piece of due diligence is to obtain a copy of a company's business licence. This will tell you the following:
1. The legal representative of the company.
2. The name and address of the company.
3. The amount of registered capital, which is also its limited liability.
4. The type of company.
5. The business scope.
6. The date the company was established and the period covered by the licence.

You should check that the information contained in the business licence matches what you already know and, if it doesn't, then find out why. You will have more security if you know who the legally responsible person is, so find out who you are dealing with.

Chapter 9: Employing Staff in South Korea

South Korea has a motivated and highly educated workforce that leads the world in a range of high-tech disciplines. Seven per cent of the country's GDP is spent on education and 74 per cent of South Koreans undertake postgraduate-level education.

You will find workers in South Korea to be disciplined, hard working and keen to undergo training. South Korea greatly values its workforce highly and is keen to attract high-quality skills from overseas. It has recently relaxed restrictions on visas for overseas workers. The organisation Contact Korea, has Korean Business Centres in 29 countries around the world, including the UK, dedicated to attracting talented people to work in South Korea.

Skills development

South Korea is keen to promote ongoing skills development. South Korea's Employee Skills Development Act exists to promote employee skills development and improve the productivity of the country's businesses.

The Ministry of Employment and Labour (MOEL) in South Korea is the body that oversees issues such as employment conditions, industrial relations, accident protection, welfare promotion, job security and vocational training.

Recruiting Channels

There are several channels for recruiting staff in South Korea. It is worth remembering that South Korea is one of the most internet enabled countries in the world – nine out of 10 homes have access to the internet and the country has the highest rates of broadband usage; so the internet is an ideal way of publicising job vacancies.

See below for the most used channels for recruiting staff:

1. Advertise jobs to UK graduates on the UK's official graduate careers website. www.prospects.ac.uk/south_korea_job_mark et.htm
2. Online job services, such as www.contactkorea.go.kr/en and http://jobs.asiabot.com
3. Classified adverts for jobs in English are available in English daily newspapers, such as The Korea Times and The Korea Herald.
4. Other newspapers (many of which have English-language pages) include: Chosun Ilbo; Dong-a Ilbo; Korea Economic Daily; Maeil Business; Hangyore Sinmun; and JoongAng Ilbo.
5. Trade journals for key industry sectors, such as Fashionbiz, M&M, VM Space, GG Game, Monthly Design and Monthly Motors.
6. Recruitment companies: South Korea is a member of the International Confederation of Private Employment Agencies (CIETT). There are many experienced domestic and

international recruitment agencies operating across the country's main business regions. Companies like Manpower, Heidrick and Struggles and Adecco have a permanent base in South Korea.

7. Contact the British Embassy, British Chamber of Commerce or educational institutes.

Recruitment process

When you are recruiting in South Korea, make sure that you carry out all the normal steps that you would if recruiting in the UK. Ensure that candidates' technical and linguistic capabilities match their claims and that you hire staff at the right level for the role.

Carry out due diligence. This includes conducting personal background checks and checking all references before offering the position.

Offer appropriate remuneration. It can be difficult to find up-to-date statistics on the going rate of pay for certain types of employment. Engineers, for example, can earn between 5 million KRW (US$4,500) a month and 8 million KRW (US$7,200).

Overseas training

Offering employees the opportunity to train overseas is also very attractive at all levels, although make sure that in return for providing such training employees make a commitment to stay with your company for a specified period of time.

A word of caution

A lot of smaller companies setting up an office in South Korea may well just employ one person to deal with all aspects of running the company. Although this may be convenient and cost-effective, it might not be the best way to run your operation.

If your employee is not familiar with the rules and regulations pertaining to running an international office or business in South Korea, then you may soon have to deal with issues of non-compliance, which could prove very costly. Moreover, having one person in control of all financial and legal aspects of the business is obviously risky.

Working hours

South Korea has one of the longest weeks in the world. Recent legislation limits the average working week in any two-week period to 40 hours and prevents workers being required to work a 12-hour day. However, this is not widely observed and most people still work late into the evening.

Standard working hours in the country are 09.00-18.00, Monday to Friday.

Public holidays

There are 15 national holidays in South Korea and most of them are observed by the majority of offices and businesses. In addition, workers accrue leave based on their attendance record and the number of years with a company.

Public holidays are:

January 1: New Year's Day

1st day of 1st lunar month: The Lunar New Year (Seolal) is the most important of the traditional Korean holidays and lasts three days.

March 1: Independence Movement Day
8th day of 4th lunar month: Buddha's Birthday (Seokka Tanshin-il)

May 5: Children's Day

June 6: Memorial Day

July 17: Constitution Day

15th day of 8th lunar month: Mid-autumn Festival (Chuseok). This is also a three-day holiday

August 15: Liberation Day

October 3: National Foundation Day

December 25: Christmas Day

Chapter 10: Sales Promotion and Media in South Korea

South Koreans tend to prefer fashion brands imported from Europe and the US over imports from other Asian countries, such as China. Luxury brands are viewed as a mark of wealth and social status.

Sales promotion

Companies that appoint local partners can usually be guided by them with regards to the type of advertising and sales promotion that would suit the launch of their product/s.

The media

South Korea is one of the few Asian nations where there is genuine news pluralism. The country has more than 100 national and local daily newspapers and readership is high. There are several terrestrial TV networks and most of the population subscribes to digital, cable and satellite. The country leads the world in high-speed and wireless internet. You may wish to work with local marketing specialists who will understand the most appropriate channels for reaching your target market.

TV and radio: South Korea has four main broadcasting companies; Korean Broadcasting System (KBS), Munhwa Broadcasting Corporation (MBC),

Seoul Broadcasting System (SBS) and Education Broadcasting System (EBS).

Most broadcast in Korean only. There are also many cable and satellite channels, including Arirang TV, Donga TV, On Game Net and MNET. Arirang TV is the main English broadcaster and some foreign news channels are available, including the BBC and CNN. KBS runs six radio networks, including KBS World Radio, while Munhwa Broadcasting Corporation also has its own radio stations. TBS eFM is the Seoul-based English language network.

Newspapers: Among the main daily newspapers are: Chosun Ilbo; JoongAng Ilbo; Dong-a Ilbo; Hangyore Sinmun; Hankook Ilbo and Munhwa Ilbo.

There are three main English-language newspapers: The Korea Herald, The Korea Times and The JoonAng Daily, which comes bundled with The International Herald Tribune.

News agency: The news agency for South Korea is Yonhap News Agency.

Internet: According to Internet World Stats, nearly 37.5 million South Koreans were online in June 2009. The country leads the world in wireless and high-speed internet. To reflect the fast-paced nature of the South Korean marketplace, and its highly sophisticated media, your marketing strategy will need to be continually reassessed, polished and refined.

Sales literature

Tradeshows and exhibitions are a good way of meeting potential new customers, but you still need to persuade them to buy your product. Sales literature to be the most effective should be in Korean and in English and you need to decide what kind of advertising is appropriate.

Product and service adaptations

You may need to adapt your product or service to meet the needs of the South Korean market. Marketing research can help you to identify any adaptations you need to make.

Brands

Koreans are brand-savvy and price conscious. They associate imported brand names and higher prices with superior quality. Consequently, Koreans will pay close attention to country of origin, particularly when shopping for clothes.

Chapter 11: Business Communications in South Korea

While English is widely spoken among international businesses in South Korea, you will generally need to employ interpreters during formal meetings and negotiations to prevent any misunderstandings.

There are two forms of interpreting

Consecutive interpreting means you speak and then your interpreter speaks; this is the usual form for meetings, discussions and negotiations.

Simultaneous interpreting involves the immediate translation of your words as you speak them. This requires special equipment and can be expensive. It is generally used only for large seminars and conferences.

Interpreting is a skill requiring professional training. Just because someone is fluent in English and Korean, does not necessarily mean that they will make a good interpreter.

If you are giving a speech or presentation, remember that the need to interpret everything will cut your speaking time approximately in half (unless using simultaneous interpreting). It is essential to ensure that the interpreter can cope with any technical or specialist terms in the presentation. If you are giving a speech, give the interpreter the text well in advance and forewarn them of any changes.

To get the best out of your interpreter

1. Hire a well-briefed professional interpreter. Though this is likely to be expensive, it will be money well spent.

2. Have your own interpreter available, even if your South Korean counterparts have one for their side. With your own interpreter, you should also be able to get some post-meeting feedback concerning the nuances of what was said (and just as importantly not said).

3. Try to involve your interpreter at every stage of your pre-meeting arrangements. The quality of interpretation will improve greatly if you provide adequate briefing on the subject matter. Ensure your interpreter understands what you are trying to achieve.

4. Speak clearly and evenly with regular breaks for interpretation. Don't ramble on for several paragraphs without pause. Your interpreter will find it hard to remember everything you have said, let alone interpret all your points. Conversely, don't speak in short phrases and unfinished sentences. Your interpreter may find it impossible to translate the meaning if you have left a sentence hanging.

5. Avoid jargon, unless you know your interpreter is familiar with the terminology.

6. Listen to how your interpreter interprets what you have just said. If you have given a lengthy explanation but the interpreter translates it into only a few words, it may be that they have not fully understood. Or they may be wary of passing on a message that is too blunt and will not be well-received by the audience.

7. Make sure that your message is getting through clearly and in a tone that will not cause resentment.

Once you have made contact with a South Korean company, it is likely that your day-to-day phone and email communication will be in English with one of the firm's English-speaking members of staff.

If you do not think the standard of English is up to scratch, you might wish to ask for parallel texts in Korean and get them translated. This could form a valuable investment.

If you are going to sign anything as obvious as it sounds; make sure you get it translated first and by an independent translator. Do not rely on your suppliers' translation and do not be pressurised into signing anything that you do not fully understand. Most breakdowns in overseas business relations occur because of fractured communications and mutual misunderstandings.

If South Korea is likely to become a significant part of your business, you may wish to consider hiring a Korean-speaking member of staff. You might also consider taking up the challenge of learning Korean yourself. However, even if you do achieve a level of fluency, an interpreter or Korean-speaking member of staff is still an essential for business meetings.

Chapter 12: Business Etiquette in South Korea

For the international business person, doing business in foreign countries brings with it cross cultural challenges. An understanding of a country's business culture, attitudes and etiquette is a useful way of establishing good interpersonal relationships which ease the business process.

It is important to spend time establishing a good working relationship and building trust with South Koreans. Sport, families and hobbies are all good topics of conversation. South Koreans may enquire about your personal life, in an attempt to establish your age and status, and to build a relationship with you. You should answer these questions honestly and openly, but without being boastful.

The South Korean market is a favourite among foreign direct investors. However, while the country's thriving economy, liberalising marketplace and widespread use of English in business makes it an appealing choice to foreign investors, there are some significant cultural differences and challenges to be aware of.

Confucian values

South Korean society operates according to Confucian values. These state that people should respect authority, respect the collective, behave virtuously, work hard and learn hard, avoid extremes and live moderately. You will find that, if you can demonstrate these qualities, you will be more successful in your business relationships.

Kibun

There is also the concept of "face" (kibun), which is found in so many Southeast Asian societies. South Koreans strive for harmony in their business and personal relationships. To prevent loss of face, they will avoid confrontation or will tell others what they want to hear rather than tackling issues head on. For example, rather than say "no", they might say "I'll try". This allows both the person making the request and the person turning it down to save face and maintains harmony in the relationship. Some Westerners can find this approach confusing.

Try rephrasing the question in different ways so you can compare the answers you get. South Koreans are very protective of their kibun, or personal dignity. If you threaten it, you risk being excluded from future decision making, so be very careful in your business negotiations and always be respectful and mindful of kibun.

Body language

Body language is an important way of showing respect towards someone older or a more senior person in South Korea, as is using their honorific title when greeting them. Keeping your legs straight and your upper body in a slight stoop denotes respect. A slight bow is also used when expressing an apology (for example, if you tread on somebody's foot). You should also bow deeply when saying goodbye and say Annyeong-hee-gaseyo.

Sneezing and blowing your nose in public is considered rude (and sometimes funny). If you have to sneeze, try to make it quiet. If you do sneeze in front of somebody, make sure you apologise.

Use both hands when giving or receiving anything (including business cards), as it is regarded as polite.

Attire

South Koreans tend to dress appropriately for their work surroundings, as you would expect in the UK or US. Black, blue and brown coloured suits are recommended. Tight skirts, low necklines and sleeveless tops should be avoided, as should shorts.

Names and titles

When addressing someone in business you should use their professional (professor, doctor, and engineer) and honorific titles.

Women in business

Although Korean attitudes to women in business are changing slowly, it is still very rare for women to hold senior positions in South Korea. Consequently, the opportunity to work with a foreign company, with more enlightened attitudes towards equality, tends to be welcomed by many professional women in the country.

Punctuality

As has already been stated, you should be punctual for meetings and leave plenty of time for your journey to avoid arriving late.

When engaged in a business relationship, you should ensure that delivery times are clear and that you act quickly to remedy any problems.

Hospitality

Hospitality is an important part of South Korean business culture. You may be invited out to dinner in a restaurant or, occasionally, in someone's home. This is considered a great honour. You should always remove your shoes, and remember to point them towards the front door.

South Korea has one of the highest rates of alcohol consumption in the world and men are expected to partake in the country's drinking culture. Getting drunk is part of the process and your hosts may even ask you to sing (try to sing something with good grace, even if it's only a nursery rhyme, as a refusal is considered rude).

If you've had enough to drink, avoid emptying your glass. If you don't want to drink, excuse yourself on medical or religious grounds. It is considered polite to fill other people's glasses rather than your own.

Dining

There are a number of rules you should observe when dining. Most of them are basic good table manners, but there are a few that are specific to South Korea. For example, you should not hold your rice or soup bowl in your hand during the meal.

Spoons and chopsticks should not be rested on any bowl or dish and you should not hold them together in one hand. When an elderly person gets up, you should also get up. Younger people should not pick up their tableware before older people.

Negotiations

South Koreans like to spend time getting to know their business associates, so don't expect important decisions to be reached in the initial meeting. Avoid becoming visibly frustrated or irritated as this could insult your host. Be patient, but firm, allow plenty of time for negotiations and remain dignified throughout.

Greeting Etiquette

When doing business in South Korea men greet each other with a slight bow sometimes accompanied with a handshake. When handshaking, the right forearm is often propped up by the left hand. Maintaining eye contact is good etiquette. In South Korean business culture, women also shake hands. Western women doing business there will need to instigate a handshake with South Korean men, as out of politeness, a hand will not be forthcoming.

Address people by their title or by their title and family name. First names can be used once a relationship has been established but wait for your South Korean counterpart to initiate this change.

You should wait for more senior personnel to offer their hand first. South Koreans prefer a softer handshake and, during the handshake, you may support your right forearm with your left hand. Some senior South Koreans consider eye contact as rude, but that's not the norm. It is advisable to make direct eye contact when addressing South Korean business professionals in order to show honesty and interest. A man greeting a South Korean business woman should wait for her to initiate a handshake, as some women prefer to bow instead. Never use your index finger to point at somebody.

Business Card Etiquette

You will need to have a good supply of business cards as it is customary to exchange these (using both hands) when meeting a business person for the first time. Be sure to treat someone's business card with respect as to do otherwise risks insulting them. Examine the card before putting it away and never write on someone's card in their presence unless they are happy for you to do so. One good tip is to ask a question based on the information on the card. Your business cards should be translated on one side into South Korean.

Gift Giving Etiquette

A part of doing business in South Korea is the exchanging of gifts. It is done to secure favours and build relationships.

Gifts are always reciprocated so bring be sure to bring some with you from your native country. Good gifts for a first visit are office items, maybe with your logo on them. After this try and bring items of beauty and craftsmanship. Foodstuffs will also be appreciated. Avoid overly expensive gifts as this will require the recipient to match the value when they reciprocate.

If offered a gift, it is good etiquette to offer some initial resistance. However, after the giver insists for the second or third time feel free to accept. Gifts are usually not opened in front of the giver, although it may be a good idea to ask if they would like you to do so.

Business Meetings

Prior to doing business in South Korean ensure you book any meetings well in advance. The most convenient times for doing business are between 10:00 a.m. to 12:00 p.m. and 2:00 p.m. to 4:00 p.m. Times of the year to avoid include holidays like the Lunar New Year (around January/February) and the Moon Festival (around September/October).

Punctuality is important in South Korea and being on time is recommended. However, business people are busy and have hectic schedules which may cause them to be late occasionally. Be courteous and do not display any negative emotions if someone is late to meet you.

When entering a meeting room, the most senior member of your delegation should enter the room first and should sit at the middle of the table.

Before doing business in South Korea understand that personal relationships generally take precedence over business. A first meeting is a 'get to know' affair rather than focusing on business matters. It could take many business trips to South Korea to reach an agreement or close a deal.

The tips above point to a few considerations one must make prior to doing business in South Korea. Cross cultural awareness in areas such as meeting etiquette and business protocol are ways of enhancing your business trip and maximizing your potential by minimising misunderstandings and promoting clear lines of communication.

Chapter 13: Regulations and Incentives

The Republic of Korea is a member of the World Trade Organization (WTO) and has signed subsidiary agreements including TRIPs (Trade Related Aspects of Intellectual Property) and the Government Procurement Agreement (GPA).

Public Procurement

The Public Procurement Service (PPS) handles the purchase of goods and incidental services required by central and sub-central government bodies, government construction contracts and stockpiling raw materials. However, not all GPA-covered procurement is handled by the PPS. Korean government-invested corporations handle procurement in-house using the same open and formal procedures required by the GPA. Potential bidders must register with the PPS at least one business day before the date the bid begins. Foreign bidders are allowed to register with the PPS prior to entering into a contract. Failure to register can mean your bid is rejected so it is a good idea to register promptly.

South Korea uses the Government e-Procurement System (GePS), which publishes details of all public procurement contracts. Bids can be viewed on the PPS website and are valid for at least 45 days after the bid opening date.

Intellectual Property

It is recommended that you register your patents and trademarks with the Korean Intellectual Property Office (KIPO) before you commit to any important deals with South Korean companies. In principle, the patent and trademark registration system in South Korea is based on which was the first company to register successfully with KIPO. Therefore, the sooner you register the better. Companies that do not register in South Korea will be disadvantaged in any future disputes over IPR.

Restrictions

Most imported goods no longer require South Korean government approval, but some products, mostly agricultural, face import restrictions, such as TRQs (Tariff-rate quotas) with prohibitive over-quota tariffs. South Korea implements quantitative restrictions through its import licensing system.

Investment rules and incentives

Definition of FDI - The South Korean government describes foreign direct investment (FDI) as "an investment made by a foreigner for the purpose of establishing a continued economic relationship with a corporation in the Republic of Korea or a business owned by a citizen of the Republic of Korea".

FDI includes: the acquisition of shares or equity from a Korean corporation or business; providing long-term loans to Korean corporations; contributing to non-profit organisations and other similar activities. FDI differs from a portfolio investment, the purpose of which is to earn margins from stock transactions for short term profits.

Imports in South Korea

With the exception of high-risk items related to public health and sanitation, national security and the environment, which often require additional documentation and technical tests, goods imported into South Korea by companies with no record of trade-law violations don't require customs inspection.

Importers can make an import declaration online using the Korean Customs Service's (KCS) Electronic Data Interchange (EDI) system for paperless import clearance. There is no need to visit the customs house.

Import declarations may be filed at the customs house before a vessel enters a port or before the goods are unloaded into bonded areas. Goods don't have to be stored in the bonded area if the import declaration is accepted.

Exporters can file an export notice to Korean Customs by computer-based shipping documents at the time of export clearance. All commodities can be freely exported unless they are included on the negative list.

Korean Customs allows free customs entry to goods brought into South Korea that are hand-carried by foreign business people (such as laptop personal computers) for use during their stay in the country. There are some exceptions, but this is rare.

Generally, Korean Customs makes a note on the traveller's passport which requires them to take the item/s out of South Korea when they depart.

Exchange controls

South Korea has liberalised foreign-exchange controls in line with OECD benchmarks. An overseas firm that invests under the terms of the Foreign Capital Promotion Act (FCPA) is permitted to remit a substantial portion of its profits, providing it submits an audited financial statement to its foreign exchange bank.

To withdraw capital, firms must present a stock valuation report issued by a recognised securities company or the Korean Appraisal Board. Foreign companies not investing under the FCPA must repatriate funds through authorised foreign-exchange banks, once they have obtained South Korean government approval. South Korea does not routinely limit the repatriation of funds, except in highly exceptional circumstances.

Chapter 14: Tax and Investment Incentives

Free economic zones

The South Korean government has established special zones, called free economic zones, in certain areas to encourage FDI. These are self-contained living and business districts, with air and sea transport, logistics, international business centres, financial services, houses, schools, hospitals, shopping and entertainment.

There are currently six free economic zones in South Korea, including:
1. Incheon.
2. Yellow Sea.
3. Saemangum/Gunsan.
4. Daegu/Gyeongbuk.
5. Gwangyang.
6. Busan/Jinhae.

Customs and regulations

There are two methods of determining a duty amount:
1. Declaration and Payment.
2. Notice of Assessment.

In Declaration and Payment, the person wanting to import goods makes a declaration on the payment of the customs duties direct to the customs house.

In Notice of Assessment, the customs house imposes and collects customs duties. In most cases, businesses use the Declaration and Payment method.

The Notice of Assessment system is mainly used for the imposition of minor customs duties, such as on passengers' and crews' goods, unaccompanied baggage and postal matters.

Related information and customs forms can be found on the Korea Customs Service website: http://english.customs.go.kr

Rules relating to FDI: FDI in South Korea is covered by the Foreign Investment Promotion Act (FIPA). This states that a foreigner may carry out investment activities in South Korea without restriction unless the investment is deemed harmful to national security, public order, the health and wellbeing of Korean nationals or Korea's environment, or unless it goes against established social morals, customs or laws.

FDI incentives: The South Korean government aims to transform the country into one of the top 10 business-friendly economies in the world by 2013. It is keen to encourage foreign investors and has been making stringent efforts to ease excessive regulations and provide incentives for FDI.

The incentives include:
  1. **Tax support:** Corporate and income tax on business income, dividends, technology introduction considerations and earned

income have been reduced for foreign firms and investors. Acquisition tax, registration tax and property tax have also been lowered.

2.   **Cash grants:** Central and local governments provide grants to foreign investors to build new factories, as long as they meet certain criteria. Among the factors taken into account are whether it is a high-tech industry or involves technology transfer and the number of jobs created.

3.   **Site location support:** Foreign investment zones are designated to attract FDI. Businesses that locate in these zones receive certain incentives.

4.   **Other support:** Land, factories and other national or public properties owned by central or local government may be used, leased or sold to foreign-invested companies through a private contract, with a lease period of up to 50 years. At the end of the lease period, the contract may be renewed for up to a further 50 years.

Chapter 15: Export, Import and Payment Terms

Import Controls

Korea runs a dual-channel system in which a traveller can choose between a red and green channel for customs clearance. As long as a traveller accurately submits his/her customs declaration to a customs official, he or she may enjoy improved service such as quick customs clearance, permission to pay duties after completing customs clearance, and other conveniences.

The customs office will confiscate items that exceed the duty/tax free allowance or those items listed as prohibited or restricted from entering the country.

Major Exports and Imports

Major Exports are automobile, wireless communication devices, semiconductor, petroleum products, ship structure and parts; liquid crystal displays (LCDs). Korea's semiconductor industry has shown remarkable growth in the past 20 years and now ranks first in the world in terms of total production in 2009.

Korea has been the largest D-RAM producer in the world since 1998 and has emerged as the world's largest manufacturer in memory semiconductor production, of which D-RAM constitutes a major portion. In the shipbuilding industry, Korea recaptured the world's no.1 title in 2004, with exports of US$15.66 billion and a ship manufacturing volume of 8.34 million compensated gross tons. In 2005, Korea held fast to the first place with exports jumping to US$17.7 billion and shipbuilding volume reaching 10.24 million compensated gross tons. And, in 2006, the shipbuilding industry recorded exports of US$ 22.1 billion. Major imports are oil, semiconductor, petroleum products, steel, and semiconductor manufacture equipment.

Export Documentation

If you are exporting to South Korea, you will need the following documents to clear Korean Customs: commercial invoice, certificate of origin, packing lists, bill of landing and maritime insurance.

As an exporter of goods you need to develop an understanding of various issues, such as:
1. The legal and regulatory requirements your consignments have to comply with.
2. The paperwork involved.
3. The right mode of transport, i.e. road, air, rail and sea.
4. Packaging and labelling.
5. How freight forwarders can help you.
6. Rules for dangerous goods.

Labelling and packaging regulations

Country-of-origin labelling is required for commercial shipments entering South Korea. Further labelling and marking requirements for specific products, such as pharmaceuticals and food, are covered by specific regulations from the South Korean government agencies responsible for these items.

South Korean-language labels, except for country of origin markings that must be shown at the time of customs clearance, can be attached locally on products in the bonded area, either before or after clearance.

The South Korea Food & Drug Administration is responsible for setting and enforcing Korean labels for food products, other than livestock products. These are regulated by the Ministry of Food, Agriculture Forestry and Fisheries which also has its own set of standards for markings for the country-of-origin labelling of agricultural products.

The South Korean Customs Service publishes a list of the country-of-origin labelling requirements by Harmonized System Code number. Local importers usually print South Korean language labels when imported quantities are not large, and can consult with the South Korean Customs Service as to where they can be attached to the product.

The Certificate of Origin should indicate the item's description, quantity, price, place of origin, exporter and importer, and be written in English, Korean or French. For items shipped directly to South Korea from their country of origin, the Certificate of Origin should be issued by the relevant customs authorities or Chamber of Commerce. The items themselves should be clearly marked with their country of origin.

Terms of payment

The payment terms you can normally expect in South Korea are "100 per cent Confirmed Irrevocable Letter of Credit," and these are the terms you should quote. You are unlikely to obtain deposits with order, or prior to shipment and it may be counterproductive to try to insist on them.

Letters of Credit are normally opened four to six weeks prior to the shipment date. The expiry date of the Letter of Credit will be geared very much to the promised delivery date. It is important, therefore, that delivery promises are fulfilled or the Letter of Credit will expire.

South Koreans usually like to deal in US dollars because this is still the predominant currency in Asia. Sterling is an acceptable currency, but for price comparison purposes a sterling price will invariably be converted to US dollars, usually at a rate that is beneficial to the buyer. You may consider it appropriate, therefore, to quote in US dollars in the first instance.

South Koreans are formidable negotiators, but they will pay a fair and competitive price. The price quoted should be on a FOB (Freight on Board) basis. South Koreans usually like to organise the shipping themselves on the basis that they can negotiate more competitive rates.

Chapter 16: Getting to South Korea

By Sea

South Korea has extensive and modern infrastructure, including major port and airport facilities. Busan is the country's largest port and the fifth-largest in the world. It is located on the south-eastern most tip of the Korean peninsula, facing the Korean Strait. Busan is well connected to Seoul and the rest of South Korea by the KTX high-speed rail system. Incheon also has a major international port at Yeongjong.

By Air

Incheon International Airport is the main gateway to South Korea. Located just over an hour west of Seoul, the airport is one of the most technologically advanced in Asia. Other international airports include Gimpo Airport, near Seoul; and Gimhae Airport, for Busan and other major cities.

Two airlines, Korean Air and Asiana Airlines, operate daily direct flights from London to Seoul (flight time around 11 hours). Incheon International Airport handles all international flights whereas Gimpo Airport handles all domestic flights and short flights to/from Tokyo, Osaka, Shanghai and Nagoya.

Getting to and from the airport

Incheon International Airport's website contains detailed information about buses, trains and taxis from the airport, including estimated times and fares to major destinations.

Travelling within South Korea

South Korea has a well-developed transport network, with good road, rail and air links. Most domestic destinations are within an hour's flight of Seoul. Korea Air, Asiana Airlines and a few domestic discount carriers handle flights within the country.

Gimpo Airport, located between the western area of Seoul and the newer Incheon International Airport, handles most domestic flights, as well as short-haul flights to Japan and China. Gimpo Airport is easily accessible via Subway Line 5 from Seoul, a journey that takes around 45 minutes. The capital has an excellent subway system, as well as buses and taxis. Gimpo Airport also has its own bus service.

Visas

There are different types of visa for people who want to work or invest in South Korea. Foreign investors need to apply for a Foreign Investment Visa, known as a D-8. To obtain a D-8 you will need to apply to the South Korean Embassy in your country.

Before you do so, you will need to appoint a Korean taxation accountant to act as your tax agent, to ensure that your taxes are paid on time. Your agent will fill in a form that has to be submitted to the immigration authorities. Anyone staying in
South Korea for more than 90 days must apply for an alien registration card.

Banking

Opening hours

Banks in South Korea are open between 09.00 to 16.00, Monday to Friday. The country's central bank is the Bank of Korea.

Local commercial banks include:
1. Hana Bank
2. Kookmin Bank
3. Korea Exchange Bank
4. Shinhan Bank
5. Woori Bank
6. Foreign commercial banks include:
7. ABN AMRO
8. Bank of America
9. Bank of Tokyo-Mitsubishi
10. Citibank
11. Deutsche Bank
12. HSBC
13. Mizuho Corporate Bank
14. SC First Bank
15. Merchant banks include:
16. Kumho Investment Bank
17. Meritz

18. Tong Yang Securities Inc.

All commercial banks are authorised foreign exchange dealers. Licensed money changers are also found in urban centres, ports, airports and major shopping complexes.

Currency

The currency of South Korea is the Korean won (KRW). A single won is divided into 100 jeon. The jeon is no longer used for everyday transactions, and appears only in foreign exchange rates. Under exchange-control rules travellers may import or export up to US$10,000 per person without prior approval. There are no limits on the amount of foreign currency (notes and/or traveller's cheques) travellers may import.

Chapter 17: Communications and Capital Market South Korea

Communications

South Korea was ranked at the top among the 181 economies considered in the digital opportunity index (DOI) published by the International Telecommunication Union. That is based on comprehensive indicators including Internet penetration rate, telecom spending-to-income ratio, and rate of Internet use.

To further upgrade its ICT infrastructure, South Korea is currently constructing BCN (Broadband Convergence Networks), the completion of which is expected to be a major stride toward achieving ubiquitous networking in South Korea, as the new networks will enable QoS (Quality of Service) guaranteed broadband multimedia services that are nearly ubiquitously accessible from anywhere in the country. South Korea is also highly competitive on the technology front. WiBro, or "Wireless Broadband" -- a high-speed portable Internet system; terrestrial wave DMB; intelligent integrated information broadcasting; standard embedded software integration technology; low-power SoC (System on Chip) for interactive DMB; and telematics wireless telecommunication integration technology are just some of the impressive technologies in the country's arsenal. These innovative technologies are expected to succeed South Korea's CDMA technology, whose total economic effect has been estimated at 56 trillion won, as powerful new engines of growth for the country's ICT sectors.

Finance

The Korean financial market consists of a financial market in the traditional sense, in which short and long-term financial products are traded in relation to procurement and operation of funds, a foreign exchange market, and a derivatives market.

Foreigners' investments into domestic securities were promoted step by step in consideration of their effect on macro economic variables, such as currency, interest rate, exchange rate, etc. Currently, foreigners may acquire all securities under the Securities Exchange Act. According to the financial services handled, financial institutions in South Korea are categorized into banks, non-bank deposit handling institutions that handle financial products similar to bank deposits, securities companies and asset management companies, insurance companies, and other financial institutions, etc.

Capital Markets Consolidation Act

With the implementation of the Capital Markets Consolidation Act in February 2009, the strictly separated fields within the existing capital market in the finance sector such as securities companies, asset management companies, merchant banks, futures companies, trust companies, etc will be consolidated.

This measure is expected to bring changes to the Korean capital market to promote financial companies cantered around investment banks and private equity funds to become larger and more specialized, as well as the expansion of derivatives' underlying assets, which will lead to Korea becoming a major financial hub.

Government Policy on Foreign Investment in South Korea

Unless otherwise stipulated by law, a foreigner may carry out foreign investment activities in South Korea without restrictions. However, restrictions are placed when the investment is deemed as harmful to national security, public order, the health and welfare of South Korean nationals, and environment preservation, or goes against established social morals, customs, and/or the laws of the Republic of Korea. Through the Foreign Investment Promotion Act, foreign investments are provided with a higher level of investment protection than indirect investments such as investments through securities and bonds. Overseas remittances of gains from the stocks acquired by foreign investors and stock transactions, principal and fees paid according to a loan contract under the Foreign Investment Promotion Act, and compensation under a technology import contract are allowed in accordance to what has been permitted and notified under the foreign investment technology import contract at the time of the remittance.

The Ministry of Strategy and Finance may temporarily suspend or restrict foreign exchange transactions, when it is unavoidably required due to force majeure (war, calamities, etc.), substantial and drastic changes to internal and external economic conditions, or other matters in proportion to such. However, a foreign investment under the Foreign Investment Promotion Act shall be an exception to the application of this clause in the Foreign Exchange Trade Act. Unless otherwise stipulated by law, the business operations of foreign investors and foreign-invested companies shall be treated equally as citizens and corporations of the Republic of Korea.

Exchange Controls

All transactions involving foreign exchange in Korea or flows of capital between Korean residents and non-residents are controlled according to the provisions of the Foreign Exchange Transactions Law. The Foreign Exchange Transactions Law applies to all domestic companies, including branches, agencies, representative offices and other offices of foreign companies operating in the Republic of Korea. In essence, inflows and outflows of foreign exchange are regulated. Under the Foreign Exchange Transactions Law, foreign exchange earnings from external transactions are regarded as coming under the jurisdiction of the Republic of Korea.

Foreign investors who comply with the notification requirements of the Foreign Investment Promotion Act are guaranteed the right to remit dividends and repatriate capital through a designated foreign exchange bank.

The Foreign Investment Promotion Act guarantees the remittance of royalties, dividends and equity owned by foreign investors, any related proceeds, and any principal and interest paid from long-term loan agreements. Any suspension of foreign exchange transactions due to restrictive measures from critical situations, such as war or domestic economic strife, will not apply to Foreign Direct Investment. Under the Foreign Exchange Transactions Law, confirmation by the head of a foreign exchange bank is required to remit such funds overseas.

Chapter 18: Business Accounting Standards in South Korea

Since the 1997 foreign exchange crisis, the Financial Supervisory Commission (FSC) of Korea has accepted the recommendations of the IMF and the World Bank to fully revise South Korean business accounting standards to fit international standards. This resulted in a shift from the legal provision-like form of the past and a birth of the current business accounting standards that adhere to the global standard. From July 2007, the Korean Accounting Institute (KAI) has been commissioned by the FSC to set, revise and interpret the business accounting standards, and has been enacting and declaring the financial accounting standards or revising existing business accounting standards by designating a serial number in the order of issues.

The financial accounting standards apply to the cases of corporations under the law on external audit on corporations, creating financial statements for external users, as well as for audits by external auditors.

Business Accounting Standards and Commercial Law and Tax Law

In South Korea, laws that regulate financial reports resulting from management activities include the Commercial Law, Tax Law, Securities Exchange Act, law on external audit on corporations, Certified

Accountant Law, business accounting standards, and the accounting auditing standards. In the Commercial Law, financial statements are listed as the balance sheet, income statement, statement of appropriation of retained earnings or deficit reconciliation statement. However, the business accounting standard adds the cash flow chart and annotations to the financial statements. The Tax Law is based on the major premise of the settlement principle of claims and obligations, and fair taxation, and is different from the financial reports under the business accounting standards based on an accrual basis and realization principle. On the other hand, recent trends have shown efforts to legislate towards narrowing the gap between business accounting and tax accounting.

External Audit Policy

The external audit policy refers to the audit policy of auditing by external accountants with no rested interest in the company being audited. The policy was established to have external auditors conduct audits independently from internal auditors to protect the interested parties such as shareholders, creditors, employees, etc. and promote sound development of companies.

According to the law on external audit of corporations, auditors consisting of certified public accountants inspect whether the financial statements created by businesses at closing were done according to the business accounting standards.

Article 2 of the enforcement ordinance of the law on external audit on corporations stipulates the object of external audits as 'corporations with 10 billion KRW or more in total assets at the end of the previous business year.' Therefore, private businesses, or business with less than 10 billion KRW or more in total assets at the end of the previous business year do not need to receive an external audit. However, the Securities Exchange Act stipulates stock-listed corporations and association registered corporations to receive external audits. Hence stock-listed corporations and association registered corporations may be the objects of an external audit even if they are not considered as such according to the law on external audit on corporations.

Introduction of the International Financial Reporting Standards

The South Korea Accounting Standards Board (KASB) declared the 'K-IFRS' in December 2007 which refers to the IFRS (International Financial Reporting Standards) having been selected as the South Korean business accounting standard GAAP. Accordingly, businesses wishing to apply the IFRS are permitted to do so from 2009. From 2011, it will become compulsory for all listed companies, including those on the KOSDAQ exchange, to apply the IFRS. However, as a way to reduce the burden on non-listed companies, the accounting standards with simple accounting methods have been enacted and applied. And, in shifting key Korean financial statements from the separate financial statement to the consolidated financial statement, business capacities will be taken into consideration to have businesses with 2 trillion won and over in assets create and provide quarterly and semi-annual consolidated financial statements from 2011, while businesses with more than 2 trillion won in assets shall do so from 2013.

Chapter 19: Corporate Tax in South Korea

South Korean taxes comprise of national and local taxes. For tax purposes, an individual is defined as either a resident or non-resident of South Korea depending on his or her residence or domicile in South Korea.

A resident is liable for income taxes on the income from sources both within and outside South Korea. A non-resident is liable for income taxes on the income derived from sources within South Korea.

Under the income tax law as it applies to individuals, income derived by both residents and non-residents is subject to composite income, capital gains, retirement income and timber income taxation. Composite income taxation includes real estate rental income, business income, dividend income, interest income, employment income, pension and annuity income, temporary property income, and other income.

This income is aggregated and taxed progressively. Currently, interest and dividends are subject to withholding tax. Non-residents are taxed on income earned within South Korea in a similar way.

A company established in South Korea under Korean law is regarded as a domestic company and liable for tax on the worldwide income whereas a foreign company is only liable for tax on its Korean-source income. A foreign company without a permanent establishment (PE) in Korea is subject to withholding tax as payments are made to it.

Fiscal Year

Taxable income is ordinarily determined by reference to the year ending 31 December, which is the standard Korean financial year. However, with the consent of the Commissioner of Taxation, taxpayers may choose a substituted accounting period for the purpose of determining taxable income. This generally applies to local branches and subsidiaries of foreign companies that adopt a different balance date.

Lodgement of returns

Taxpayers are required to lodge returns annually.

Corporate Tax

There are three types of taxable income falling under corporation tax:

1. **Annual income:** Refers to the remaining balance following the deduction of exclusions for each fiscal year.
2. **Liquidation income:** Refers to the residual property value of a dissolved (merged or divided) corporation exceeding the total equity capital.
3. **Capital gains from the transfer of land:** Refers to additional tax on transfer gains from the transfer of real estate, particular houses, or land for non-business purposes

in areas in which land value has increased drastically. In this case, a tax is levied to suppress speculation, and is thus added on to the transfer gains.

Therefore, corporate tax on the income of each fiscal year, and the corporate tax on capital gains from the transfer of land, etc. overlap to form double taxation.

Taxable Income

The calculation of taxable income for a corporation is similar to the calculation of income before corporate income taxes as shown on the financial statements. The accrual basis of accounting is used in both cases. However, certain adjustments to book income will be required to derive taxable income.

Taxable income is defined as assessable income less allowable deductions. Assessable income is simply gross income adjusted to include receipts deemed to be income by the Corporate Income Tax Law and to remove tax-exempt income items. Allowable deductions include most expenses recognized for financial accounting purposes.

Corporate Tax Rate

1. KRW 200 million or less 11% of tax base.
2. More than KRW 200 million 22% of the amount in excess of KRW 200 million.

Dividends

Ninety percent of the dividend income institutional investors receive from listed corporations defined under the Securities and Exchange Act (i.e. Korea Stock Exchange-listed corporations or KOSDAQ-registered corporations), is not included in the taxable income.

If a "financial holding company" as defined under the Financial Holding Company Law, or other "holding companies" declared to the Korean Fair Trade Commission whose shareholding in their subsidiaries equals 50 percent or more of the subsidiaries' total assets (30 percent or more in the case of listed companies, 20 percent or more in the case of venture companies), receives dividends from its subsidiary, a certain percentage of the dividend will be deducted from the holding company's taxable income. These deductions are said to be dividends received deductions (DRD).

Law, "asset liquidation companies" as per the Asset Liquidation Control Law, "corporate restructuring investment companies" as per the Corporate Restructuring Investment Company Law, and "real estate investment companies" for corporate restructuring purposes as per the Real Estate Investment Company Law, distribute dividends equivalent to 90 percent or more of their profits as defined under Article 86-2-1 of the Presidential Decree, such dividends are deductible from taxable income.

94

Corporate entities other than those mentioned above are also entitled to similar benefits in proportion to their shareholding in their subsidiaries. Where the subsidiary is wholly owned, 100 percent of the income received from the subsidiary is not included in taxable income.

Where the shareholding in the subsidiary exceeds 50 percent (30 percent in the case of listed companies), 50 percent of the dividend received is not included in the taxable income.

Where the shareholding is 50 percent or less (30 percent in the case of listed companies), 30 percent of the dividend received is not included in the taxable income.

Exempt Income

Income derived from property held in trust for the benefit of the public is not subject to corporate income tax without the submission of an application for an exemption. Expenses incurred in deriving this income will not be deductible.

Interest deductions

Interest paid on loans and other debts is deductible to the extent it relates to borrowings made for income producing purposes. Thin capitalisation rules apply to reduce the deduction available where the taxpayer is a foreign entity operating in South Korea, a foreign controlled South Korean entity or a South Korean resident with foreign business investments. In each of these cases, the tax deduction for interest may be reduced if the taxpayer's debt exceeds the levels permitted under the thin capitalisation provisions.

Losses

Tax losses can be carried forward for a maximum of five years. Only tax losses of small and medium-sized companies can be carried back for a year and the company can claim a refund of tax paid in the previous year.

Grouping / Consolidation

Consolidated group may calculate taxable income as if the consolidated group is one entity. (Applicable from the fiscal year starting on or after Jan. 1, 2010).

Tax Return and Payment

Annual corporate income tax returns must be filed and corporate income tax payments must be made within three months from the end of fiscal year. If the amount of corporate income tax payable is over KRW10 million, part of the amount of tax payable must be paid in instalments within one month (2 months in case of small and medium sized corporation) from the due date of payment.

Interim Corporate Income Tax Return

A corporation subject to corporate income tax during the preceding financial year or a corporation whose current financial year exceeds six months is required to file an interim corporate income tax return for the six-month period and remit the appropriate tax payment by the end of the second month immediately following the end of the interim period (i.e. six fiscal months). The interim corporate income tax paid will be credited against the annual corporate income tax payable.

Chapter 20: Personal Income and Capital Gain Tax in South Korea

Interaction with International Tax Regime

The International Tax Coordination Law prioritises the South Korean Double Tax Agreements (DTAs) over the domestic tax law. The South Korean tax authority may exchange tax information with its concerned contracting states (those countries who have concluded DTAs with Korea), subject to the provisions and limitation of the DTAs.

As of December 2008, Korea has entered into bilateral DTAs with 70 countries. Whilst the primary objective of the DTAs is the avoidance of international double taxation, these DTAs serve to promote the introduction of advanced technology and capital from abroad, as well as encourage business expansion of domestic companies in foreign countries.

These DTAs are intended to reduce or eliminate double taxation, deal with administrative matters, and promote closer economic cooperation. The DTAs apply to individuals and corporations alike, but the impact on corporate income tax is more complex.

Generally, the DTAs provide rules for determining the income that each country has the right to tax. This allocation of income will depend on factors such as the residency of the earner and the source of the income. Most DTAs provide for foreign tax credits, which help to reduce the tax liability in cases where both countries have the right to tax the same income items. Each DTA generally delineates the circumstances where income arises in the other country. Finally, most DTAs reduce the withholding taxes on payments of dividends, interest and royalties flowing between South Korea and the treaty partner.

Branch Tax

If the treaty between South Korea and the foreign country allows the imposition of a branch profits tax, the tax is imposed on the "adjusted taxable income" of the South Korean branch of the foreign corporation. 25 percent (or at a reduced rate as provided in the treaty) of the adjusted taxable income of a foreign corporation is levied as a branch profits tax in addition to corporate income tax. The adjusted taxable income is calculated by deducting regular corporate income tax and the resident tax from the taxable income.

In addition, where the net assets at the end of the taxable year exceed the net assets at the beginning of the taxable year, the excess amount is allowed as a deduction in computing taxable income.

Personal Income Tax

Personal Income Tax is imposed on the global income and scheduler income of an individual. Global income refers to interest, dividends, real estate rental income, business income, wages and salaries, temporary property income, pension income, and other income, and scheduler income denotes retirement income, capital gains, and timber income. Resident individuals are taxed on their worldwide income. Non-resident individuals are taxed only on South Korean-source income. A non-resident is liable for tax only on the income derived from South Korea and there are two methods of taxation; composite income taxation and withholding taxation.

The composite income taxation is applied to non-resident taxpayers with their business places in South Korea or income incurred from real estate located in South Korea (excluding capital gains from the transfer of land or buildings). For those non-residents with no business places in South Korea or income incurred from real estate located in South Korea, withholding taxation is applied.

Capital Gains Tax

The capital gains tax applies to the income accruing from the transfer of certain assets by an individual in a given year. 'Transfer' under tax law refers to the de facto transfer for the value of assets arising from sale, exchange, capital contribution in kind to a corporation, etc. whether or not such transfer or assets are registered. A corporation is not subject to capital gains tax, and is instead taxed on income generated from this transfer in a form of corporate tax.

Real Property and Property of its kind

If lands, real-estates or other properties are transferred, the capital gains tax shall be prorated according to the period of possession. For example, 50 percent for less than one year, 40 percent for one year to less than two years, and 9 percent to 36 percent for more than 2 years. In case the property is transferred before owner's registration, the tax rate will be 70 percent. For specific share transfers, the holdings of a corporation that possesses excessive real property, such the rights to use specific facilities (golf club membership, etc.), and business rights, a tax rate of 9 percent to 36 percent shall be applied regardless of the period of possession.

Specific Shares
1. Value of real property is more than 50% of a corporation's total asset value.
2. Majority shareholder owns 50% or more of the total interest.
3. The stock transfer ratio is more than 50%.

The equity securities of a corporation that possesses real property excessively
1. The value of real property accounts for more than 80% of the total asset value.
2. The shares of a corporation that built or acquired and is operating or renting one or more of the following:
   a. golf
   b. courses
   c. ski resorts
   d. condominiums

e.   specialized resort facilities.

Equity Securities

In case of the unlisted shares, if a major stockholder of a large corporation transfers them after retaining less than a year, a tax rate of 30 percent shall be applied. If such stocks are retained for more than a year, a tax rate of 20 percent is applied. Minority stockholders of large corporations transferring unlisted stocks, shall be liable to a 20 percent rate, regardless of the period retained. If a small and medium corporation transfers its unlisted stocks, they will be liable to 10 percent tax, regardless of its period retained. Listed stockholders, in principle, are normally not subject to tax. If, however, a majority shareholder transfers them after holding on to them for less than a year, he or she will be liable to a 30 percent rate of tax. If he or she retains the stocks for more than a year, the tax will be 20 percent.

Value Added Tax

Value Added Tax (VAT) is a tax levied on added value in each step of production and distribution. In principle, VAT is a general consumption tax levied on the consumption of all goods and services, and at the same time, a form of indirect tax for which the transfer of tax burden can be anticipated. VAT takes the form as a multi-level taxation method by taxing added value created in each step of the transaction. Goods and services for basic life necessities, education, and medical services are subject to exemption.

Taxation and Tax Rates Tax Refund System Proxy Payment System

1. Value-added tax will be collected where a trader supplies goods or services. The rate of value-added tax is 10%, and the trader shall be provided a tax invoice. The amount payable is output tax-input tax to be deducted.

2. Goods for export; services rendered outside South Korea; and other goods or services supplied for foreign exchanges earnings are zero-rated and the related input taxes incurred are refundable.

3. A non-resident without a domestic establishment and a recipient of a service from a foreign corporation should pay VAT on the payment for the taxable services.

Composite Real Estate Tax

With the government's revised plan of the real-estate possession tax (2003) by the government, the Composite Real Estate Act was prepared, and as a part of the activities, the concept of composite real estate tax was introduced. Put into effect in 2005, the policy aims to reinforce taxation on excessive real estate owners, suppress real estate speculation, reorganize irrational aspects of the local tax system.

In regard to property tax, the relevant local government in reference to the address of a land/ building owners shall levy taxes on the land and buildings in their district. Taxation is done after adding together the total number of properties owned by an individual household. However, composite real tax can change every year according to changes in real-estate policy. Therefore, it is advised that the Composite Real Estate Act be referred to, and the accurate standards of assessment and tax rate checked.

Local Taxes

Local taxes consist of provincial, city and county taxes.

1. Provincial taxes include acquisition tax, registration tax, race tax, horse race tax, license tax, community facility tax and local education tax.
2. City or county taxes include inhabitant tax, property tax, mileage tax, automobile tax, agricultural income tax, butchery tax, urban planning tax, and business place tax. At the same time, local education tax is added to taxes such as registration tax and property tax.

Acquisition Tax

Persons acquiring the following are liable to being taxed within 30 days of acquisition:

1. Real estate (land, buildings)
2. Motor vehicles, heavy equipment (heavy equipment for construction according to the Construction Machinery Management Act)
3. Golf club, condominium, and health club memberships, etc.

Generally, the tax base is two percent of the acquisition price. However, a high tax is levied for the acquisition of luxury properties, etc.

Registration Tax

Registration tax refers to tax levied on items related to the acquisition, transfer, change or cancellation of property rights and other rights are officially registered or recorded. The standards of registration tax assessment are the price, credit amount, or investment amount at the time of registering/recording the rights, etc.

Property Tax

Property tax is a city, county, or ward tax levied on the owners of land, buildings, boats, and/or airplanes for private use. The object for taxation for land is divided into the aggregate summing up of taxation objects, special summing up taxation objects, and separate taxation objects.

1. Aggregate summing up taxation objects: Land other than objects of special summing up taxation objects, and separate taxation objects.
2. Special summing up taxation objects: Land attached to buildings that have been calculated by using a certain ratio of ownership by the taxpayer on the basic date for taxation, and land with cause to be objects of special summing up taxation.
3. Separate taxation objects: Farms, fields, fruit orchards, ranch lands, forest lands, private golf courses and other legally appointed lands.

The standard of assessment of property tax is the statutory standard price of fair market value.

Resident Tax

Residential tax is largely divided into per capita rate and per income rate. Per capita rate levies an equal amount of tax on individuals, offices, and corporations with business locations located within city limits. Per income rate levies tax by utilizing income tax, corporation tax, and agricultural income tax as the standard of assessment.

The object of residents' tax and the tax amount is as follows. The city mayor or county magistrate may increase or decrease the tax rate via regulation by up to 50% of the standard tax rate.

Business Place Tax

The business place tax is levied on those with places of business in cities or counties to supply costs required for environmental improvement and maintenance. Business place tax is divided between the per property rate and the per employee rate, and is exempted for business with less than 50 employees. When the Business place taxpayer has not paid the declared amount by the due date for payment, or has paid insufficiently, 20% of the unpaid tax, or insufficient tax shall be added on to be collected.

Chapter 21: Other Taxation in South Korea

Tariff Assessment

All goods being imported from foreign countries cannot be brought into South Korea unless their customs duties are prepaid. Customs duties are calculated by multiplying tax base of the tariff tax base by the tariff rate.

The tariff tax base is either the value of the imported goods or the quantity. The tariff rate is provided on the tariff rate table by group of items. As the tax rate applies to each HS Number corresponding to an item or a group of items, the tariff is affected by the decision on which value should be regarded as the taxable value or how the taxable value is decided.

If the value is the tax base of the tariff, it is an "ad valorem duty" and if the quantity is tax based, it is called a "specific commercial duty." The value, which is the tax base of the ad valorem duty, is called the "taxable value." South Korean customs valuations on taxable values reflect the relevant provisions of the WTO Valuation Agreement and have the same principals of the international tariff valuation.

Cases not recognized as sales

1. Goods imported free of charge.

2. Goods imported for consignment sale where sale prices are determined by auctions etc.
3. Goods imported to be sold in the local market under the exporter's responsibility.
4. Goods imported by legally dependent entities such as branch offices etc.
5. Goods imported under a lease agreement.
6. Imported goods for gratuitous lease.
7. Goods imported to be disposed within South Korea at the consignor's expense (such as industrial waste etc.)
8. Imported goods with restriction for their use and dealings.

Inheritance and Gift Taxes

Individuals and non-profit companies that acquire property through inheritance or bequest are liable for Inheritance Tax. A gift tax is payable by resident beneficiaries and non-resident beneficiaries who receive property located in South Korea. Both taxes are imposed at varying rates based on the tax value of the property.

Education Tax

Education tax is a tax levied upon the income of persons engaged in the banking and insurance businesses and various taxes such as surtax.

Stamp Tax

The stamp tax is levied on a person who prepares a document certifying establishment, transfer, or change of rights to property.

Securities Transaction Tax

The Securities Transaction Tax (STT) is levied when the securities are transferred. The basic tax rate of STT is 0.5 percent and elasticity tax rates of STT are 0.15 percent to 0.3 percent. In case of listed stocks, the taxpayers are securities settlement corporations and securities companies. In case of unlisted stocks, the taxpayer is the transferor. However, in the case that a non-resident foreign corporation, whose business place is not within the country transfers securities, the purchaser of the securities must withhold taxes from the purchase price on a securities transaction certificate, and the location of the main office of the corporation that issued the securities becomes location responsible for tax payment.

Repatriation of Profits and Transfer Pricing

In addition to paying interest and dividends, the payment of management fees, service fees and royalties are methods of repatriating profits to the non-resident associates, controllers and owners of foreign entities. In these circumstances, the payments made by the foreign resident to the non-resident associate must reflect the market value of the goods and/or services to the South Korean company, that is, all payments must be calculated with reference to arm's length market rates.

Where the South Korean Tax Office takes the view that the South Korean company has paid an excessive amount for the goods and/or services, the South Korean Tax Office can disallow the deduction claimed by the South Korean company, and substitute an alternative price.

Other transactions between South Korean taxable entities (or branches), and their related foreign entities or head offices are also subject to the transfer pricing rules.

Where South Korean branch of a foreign company remits profits to its parent by way of management fees or service fees, the profits are subject to 5-15% of branch profits tax depending on foreign countries.

Chapter 22: Grants and Incentives

Tax incentives are provided under the special tax treatment control law (STTCL). There are a number of tax incentives in South Korea related to a small and medium enterprise's business performance, international capital movement, investment promotion, business restructuring, public business promotion and foreigners' investment etc.

Tax Support for Foreign-Invested Companies

According to the Tax Exemptions and Exceptions Act, corporate and income tax on business income, dividends income, technology introduction considerations, earned income, etc. has been reduced. Acquisition tax, registration tax, and property tax have been reduced for properties that have been acquired or held.

Corporate Tax Reduction

Reduction in corporate tax for foreign-invested companies applies to income from businesses qualifying for reductions under the Tax Exemptions and Exceptions Act. However, in the case that a South Korean citizen (corporation) directly or indirectly holds 10% or more of the voting shares of a foreign corporation or foreign business that has invested in a business subject to tax reduction, the portion of the investment proportionate to the ratio of the said held shares will not be subject to tax reduction.

That is to say, the tax reduction shall not apply to domestic round trips of domestic companies that have advanced overseas. The initial day of reckoning tax reductions is, whichever is sooner between, the tax year in which the first income is created, or the tax year in which the 5th year anniversary of the date of business commencement falls.

In capital increases, the date marking the registration of capital increase shall be considered the date of commencing business in applying this regulation. For foreign acquisition of shares through capitalization of reserves, revaluation reserve, etc. the period and rate of reduction shall be determined by cases of reductions for shares, etc. that are the basis of such occurrence.

If an application for tax reduction is made after increasing the capital less than 5 years after the decrease in paid-in capital, the reduction shall be determined only for the foreign investment ratio of the portion that is purely increased from before the capital decrease. However, in the case that a purely domestic company receives an investment from a foreigner through a capital increase and becomes a foreign-invested company shall be considered as a new foreign investment, and not as a case of capital increase as described above.

Local Tax (acquisition/registration/property tax) Reduction

Property acquired or held by a foreign-invested company to do business subject to reduction shall receive either a 100% or 50% reduction in acquisition, registration, and property taxes, or the items will be deducted from the standard of assessment. The amount of foreign investment ratio (for tax amount subject to reduction) multiplied by the calculated tax amount shall be deducted 100% from acquisition, registration, and property taxes for 3-5 years following the commencement of business, and 50% for 2 years afterwards on properties that have been acquired following the commencement of business operations.

However, acquisition, registration, and property taxes that have been already paid on properties that have been acquired following the commencement of business operations, but prior to becoming the subject of tax reduction, may not be refunded.

However, acquisition, registration, and property taxes on properties that have been acquired prior to the starting date of business shall be subject to 100% reduction on the tax reduction amount for properties that have been acquired following the date of the tax reduction decision. Property tax shall be subject to 100% reduction of the tax reduction amount for 3-5 years following the acquisition of the property, and 50% of the tax reduction amount for the next 2 years. According to the regulations, the local tax reduction period may be extended up to 15 years, or the reduction or deduction rate could be increased.

Exemption of Customs Tariffs, etc.

According to the Tax Exemptions and Exceptions Act, customs tariffs, etc. shall be exempted for the following capital goods used directly in businesses subject to reduction in corporate tax or income tax, and are imported through foreign investment notification on acquisition of newly issued shares, etc.
1. Capital goods imported as external or internal payment vehicles invested by foreign investors to foreign-invested companies.
2. Capital goods imported as investment objects by foreign investors.

Tax Support for Dividends

Dividends received by foreign investors from foreign-invested corporations operating tax reduction businesses are subject to tax reductions in the same rate as the portion of the amount of income of the tax reduction business, based on the dividend income during the reduction period.

Cash Grant

For foreign investments that meet certain requirements, the government and the local government shall provide cash grant for funds required to build new factories. In doing so, various aspects shall be considered regarding the foreign investment, such as whether or not they come with high technologies, effects of investment's technology transfer, the number of jobs created, redundancy with internal investments, adequacy of location, etc.

Eligibility

To become eligible for cash grant, the foreign investment ratio shall be over 30% and meet the following requirements:
1. 10 million USD and offer of foreign investment in industry support services, businesses with high technologies, or parts, material manufacturing Greenfield investment (newly built/expanded factory facilities).
2. Newly built/expanded R&D facilities in fields related to industry support services or hi-tech businesses, or research facilities of non-profit corporations invested by foreigners (10 or more full-time hired research personnel).
3. For cases when the investment amount, etc. do not meet the requirements, but has a profound impact on the domestic economy, the Foreign Investment Committee shall deliberate on the matter and determine whether the case is eligible for cash grant.
4. Establishing regional headquarters of multi-national companies (multi-national companies with business presence in 3 or more countries, and controlling regions of 2 or more countries).
5. Contributing to regional economic development as a regional strategic industry.
6. Providing items or services not produced domestically, or which can improve domestic

117

industry's competitiveness through introduction of advanced technologies.

Grant Rate

Through negotiations, the cash grant ratio shall be determined at 5% and higher of the FDI, with the upper limit determined by a closed formula. As for an R&D centre, FDI and R&D funds from overseas that are used for stipulated purposes shall be included in the funds to be calculated (except for funds raised domestically).

Legal Usage

Foreign-invested companies may use cash grant only for the following purposes:
1. Funds to support employment and training.
2. Land purchase lease.
3. Construction costs.
4. Foundation facilities installation cost.
5. Capital goods/research equipment purchasing costs.

In such cases, the purchasing amount of leased land for foreign-invested companies shall be included in the cash grant limit. However, receiving cash grant shall nullify the eligibility to be provided with leased land, or support for difference in sales price through the existing location support policy (within 50% of foreign invested amount).

Cash Grant Post-Management

Applicants' Obligations

The applicant shall, directly or indirectly, manage foreign-invested companies and faithfully carry out the obligations of the cash grant contract, as well as the investment expenditure plan. The applicant shall enter into insurances, or take other similar measures to make it possible to recover and replace, to a satisfactory level, all assets (including those under construction) such as building, facilities and equipment, etc.

Contracts for acquiring assets that receive cash grants shall be concluded in a way that utilizes the cash grant fund in the most efficient way through public tenders, official appraisals, request for 2 or more estimate, etc. Prior written consent of the Ministry of Knowledge Economy shall be secured to use the cash supported assets for purposes other than the stated business, or to transfer, exchange, loan, or provide as collateral.
Also, the cash grant shall not be dealt out as dividends or royalties. The concerned foreign-invested companies may not give security for any liabilities than for business purposes.

During the contract period, the applicant shall provide enough information to check on the performance of the contract and submit every year to the Ministry of Knowledge Economy a statement of accounts audited externally.

Chapter 23: Intellectual Property Rights

Since concluding the 'Trade-Related Intellectual Property Rights' (TRIPs) in the Uruguay Round of the WTO negotiations, South Korea has made continuous efforts to strengthen protection of IPR by revising all related domestic laws, enacting the Intellectual Property Rights Act, and establishing the long-term government-led realization of "IPR Powerhouse Korea." Also, South Korea is making strides to expand and fortifying international cooperation for IPR protection by strengthening multilateral/bilateral cooperation, as well as cooperation between South Korea, China and Japan.

IPR can be defined as rights endowed by law on creations of human intellect that are worthy of legal protection. As is the case with ownership, which one can exercise property rights to use it directly or lend it to someone else and receive considerations from it, IPR receives certain protection set by the law to establish or transfer the rights to exercise that can be used directly, or lent to another party for use. IPR is largely divided into industrial property rights, copyrights, and new intellectual property rights.

Here, we focus on explaining the application and registration procedures of patents, utility models, trademarks, designs, and copyrights, which are industrial rights.

Patents

Patent rights go through a variety of examination procedures to be registered. The first step is to submit an application for patents under the Patent Law set by the commissioner of the Korea Intellectual Property Office (KIPO). The commissioner of KIPO must publicize the application in an official patent report 18 months following the patent application date, or prior to that when requested by the applicant. When the application is publicized, the applicant may exercise the rights valid for patents such as warnings to third parties, claims for compensation, etc. However, the rights to claim compensation may only be exercised after the patent is registered, and shall be claimed within 3 years of the registration. The applicant shall request examination within 5 years of submitting the application. If not, the application shall be considered void.

Utility Model Rights

Utility model rights apply only to those whose patent application was filed prior to September 30, 2006. Applications placed after October 1, 2006 shall apply equally as patents. After the KIPO commissioner completes the examination of methods and basic requirements, the registration creation is carried out and the registration notification is made on a utility model official report. The commissioner then provides the applied documents and their annexed articles for public viewing for 3 months following the registration notification.

Legal protection is provided to utility models for 10 years after the registration creation. And with the pre-registration non-examination policy, the registration certificate can be attained through the method and basic requirement examinations 3-6 months after the application is filed.

Trademarks

Trademarks are largely divided into trademarks, service marks, collective marks, business emblems, and are protected by the Trademarks Law. In order to be protected by the Trademarks Law in Korea, the trademark has to be registered at KIPO. The Trademarks Law prevents registration of trademarks identical, or similar to unregistered prominent trademarks. However, Trademarks Law protection does not extend to others using identical or similar trademarks, as such protection may only be provided by the Unfair Competition Prevention Act.

The trademark is valid for 10 years from the registration creation date of the trademark. The validity can be extended by 10 years through validity renewal registration application, etc. and is practically semi-permanent.

Design

Designs are easy to copy, subject to trends, and thus, are subject to particular policies that differ from other industrial property rights laws. For example, the 'non-examination registration policy (when stipulated as articles under the Design Law) applies to items that are easy to copy and are very trendy, while the 'similar design policy' can register a modified version of a basic design as a similar design. The 'one-set item design policy' makes it possible to register a single design for multiple items combined as a single set, while the 'secret design policy' allows the design to be kept secret and not publicized for 3 years after the creation of registration for design rights have been carried out, upon request from the applier. Design rights registered are protected for 15 years from the creation of the registration.

Originally, the copyright belongs to the creator upon creation. However, such creations are subjective and are difficult to understand from outside. Hence, through the copyright registration procedure of the Copyright Deliberation and Mediation Committee, various legal forces can be gained.

Registering copyrights refers to the registration of certain items related to copyright materials such as the name of the author, etc. and making it public to enable the general public to view the details. At the same time, legal forces, such as presumptive and opposing powers, are endowed to certain registered items. The registration is initiated through the application of the applicant, or the commissioning of a related institution. The order of the matters is receipt, examination, approval, registration, issuance of registration certificate, and issuance of registration official report. The Copyright Deliberation and Mediation Committee is an institution established under the Copyright Law which oversees the registration of copyrights, and is in charge of providing copyright-related materials and mediating copyright-related disputes.

Chapter 24: Employment for Foreigners and Visa

The scope of activities and employment opportunities for foreigners is relatively limited. Therefore, foreigners are limited to the scope of activities and period of stay as stated in their visa.

When looking for employment opportunities in South Korea, foreigners must obtain the proper visa status and are limited to working at the workplace specified in their visa application. When looking to change a place of employment, foreigners have to notify the Seoul Immigration Office and obtain permission to do so in advance.

South Korean Labour Law

South Korean Labour law issues are often the ones which any foreign investor conducting business in South Korean market has most difficulty in understanding. We set forth below certain basic concepts of South Korean labour law requirements.

The basic law in South Korea regulating labour standards is the Labour Standards Act (LSA), which is applicable to an employer with at least 5 employees. LSA was substantially amended September of 2003 to be more in line with international standards, and the key changes resulting from the amendment include the reduction of work hours per week from 44 hours

to 40 hours and abolishment of monthly-leave system, among other things.
Visa

In principle, a foreign national may enter the country after receiving a visa in advance from an overseas Korean embassy. A visa is a proof in recognition of permission to enter the country.

There are the following 3 ways for foreign nationals to enter the country:
1. Entering without a visa and being granted a visa and period of stay through airport entry formalities.
2. Entering the country after having a visa issued by an overseas Korean embassy or legation.
3. If for some reason an overseas embassy or legation does not have the right to issue a visa, a visa issue confirmation certificate (or confirmation number) must be obtained in advance from the immigration office nearest the Korean inviter's address and forwarded to the foreign national who may present it to the relevant officials at an overseas South Korean embassy or legation in order to receive a visa to enter the country.

All foreign nationals entering the country shall have a visa as dictated by Presidential Decree (Immigration Management Act, Article 10). South Korean visas are categorized into 36 categories according to the scope of activities. Foreign investors and essential specialists are eligible to receive a D-8 visa which designates the holder as a foreign investor.

One's sojourn in South Korea is categorized into short-term (up to 89 days) and long-term (90 days or longer). Application for a change in one's visa status to a long-term stay is granted selectively, depending on the applicant's status of sojourn. The issuance of short-term visas is swiftly issued by overseas South Korean embassies by the commissioned authority of the consul. However, long-term visas which are not commissioned must be issued by an overseas South Korean embassy or legation with the approval of the Ministry of Justice, and hence may take longer to process.

Permission of Change in Visa Status

For applicants who are eligible for a D-8 visa (those who have established a foreign invested company) to enter the country on a short-term visa or without a visa, his/her family members, and/or domestic helpers may apply for a change in visa status. Applications for permission to change one's visa status may be processed at the local immigration office or at Invest KOREA within the permitted period of sojourn, and a change permit to a D-8 visa will be granted.

However, permission to change visa status shall not be granted to the following:
1. Chinese nationals who enter Korea as a member of a tour group on a short-term (C-3)
2. Visa, individuals who have entered the country purely for tourism reasons.
3. Those with Visas for study (D-2).
4. Those with industrial training (D-3).

5. Those with training employment (E-8).
6. Those with non-expertise employment (E-9)/
7. Other (G-1) and tourism employment (H-1) visas.

Alien Registration

Applicants who enter the country on a long-term visa (not less than 91 days) shall apply for an alien registration card at the local immigration office within 90 days of entering the country.

Applicants who have obtained permission for a change in the status of sojourn to D-8, F-3 and F-1 after entering South Korea on a short-term visa shall immediately apply for registration at the local immigration office.

Upon leaving South Korea permanently, foreign nationals shall return his/her alien registration card to an immigration officer handling exit procedures at the port or airport of departure.

Extension of Sojourn

Business investment visa holders who wish to extend their sojourn shall apply for an extension of sojourn at the local immigration office before the expiration of the granted sojourn. Generally, the applications are made 2 months prior to expiration, or earlier when unavoidable reasons are stated, such as overseas trips, etc.

According to the size of the invested company, investment amount, operating performance, etc. a maximum of 5 years may be granted when extending the period of stay. When wishing to continue to conduct business activities or dispatch operations, a foreign investor may extend the period of stay for an unlimited number of times only if he or she has not committed any illegal activities.

Re-entry Permit

Business investment visa holders who wish to exit the country temporarily during their domestic sojourn and then re-enter the country during the same period of sojourn shall apply for a single or multiple re-entry permit at the local immigration office or at Invest KOREA.

The re-entry permit application may also be made at a port/airport immigration office when exiting the country. The re-entry permit may be granted within the time limit of passport validity, visa validity, re-entry permit validity (1 year for single-entry, 2 years for multiple-entry, and 1 year for China). However, investors whose investments total larger than US$500,000 in addition to executives of foreign-invested companies may receive re-entry permits good for up to 3 years.

Notification on Change to Place of Stay

When holders of business investment visas change their place of stay, they must notify the change of address within 14 days of moving in to the local immigration office or to the city/county/district office where the new place of stay is located.

Those failing to notify a change in the place of stay within 14 days of changing the place of stay are subject to a fine under Article 36 of the Immigration Act.

Notification on Change in Alien Registration

Business investment visa holders shall notify a change in the following to the local immigration office within 14 days:
1. Name
2. Gender
3. Date of birth, or nationality
4. Passport number
5. Date of issue and expiration date
6. Company name (in the case of a business investment)

Those failing to notify one of the above changes are subject to a fine under Article 36 of the Immigration Act.

Activities other than Status of Sojourn

When a business investment visa holder wishes to be active in activities that qualify for other than status of sojourn while being active in status of sojourn activities, the person shall apply at the local immigration office prior to conducting the activities in order to be granted permission.

Change and Addition of Work Place

Holders of business investment visas wishing to change or add a work place within the scope of their status of sojourn shall apply to the local immigration office prior to changing or adding a work place to receive permission. However, this is limited only to holders of business investment visas changing or adding a work place that is within the same group of subsidiaries.

Granting of Permanent Residence (F-5 visa)

Permanent residence visas are granted to foreign investors, executives of multinational companies in South Korea, etc. whose efforts have contributed to improving foreign investment and strengthening national competitiveness by way of attracting multinational companies to South Korea, etc.

Barring those subject to forcible deportation, permanent residences visa is granted to those who qualify for one of the following:

1. A foreign investor with investments of over US$2 million which hires 5 or more South Korean nationals.

2. A foreign investor with investments of at least US$500,000, staying 3 or more years in South Korea with an investment visa, who hires 3 or more South Korean nationals.

3. A foreign investor with investments of at least US$300,000, staying 5 years and longer in

133

South Korea with an investment visa, who hires 3 or more South Korean nationals, and who has fulfilled certain additional requirements including passing level 3 on the KICE-administered Korean proficiency exam or having a certain level of income for the last 3 years.

Benefits for holders of permanent residency

1. Exemption from the obligation to apply for extension of the period of sojourn as long as he/she maintains F-5 status.
2. Unrestricted business activities.
3. Exemption from the obligation to apply for a re-entry permit for overseas travel (when he/she enters within one year).

Permission to Hire Foreign Domestic Helpers

In order to improve the convenience of sojourn in South Korea for large-scale investors, the hiring of foreign domestic helpers is permitted. One of the following requirements shall be met to hire a foreign domestic helper:

1. A foreign investor who has invested not less than US$500,000.
2. Executives dispatched to foreign-invested corporations whose investment is not less than US$500,000.

One domestic helper per foreign investor is permitted. Even if the domestic helper enters the country with a general short-term (C-8) visa due to unavoidable reasons, he/she may apply for a change in visa status to F-1 status (visit/family). When the relationship between the domestic helper and the employer ends due to conclusion/cancellation of the employment contract, loss of business investment visa by the employer, etc. the domestic helper must exit the country.

Chapter 25: ICT Sector in South Korea

The South Korean government continues to stimulate exporting and attract foreign companies by fostering economies identified as the new growth engines in 'Green technology', 'High-tech convergence' and 'Value added service'.

South Korea has a predicted GDP growth of 3.5 per cent in 2012. South Korea has a population of 50 million and is ranked 8th in the 'Ease of Doing Business 2012' report by The World Bank.

The ICT sector is significant and very developed in South Korea. The IT sector accounts for 28% of the nation's total export and the country has become one of the leading information economies in the world. South Korea is the number one market for manufacturing of LCD (Liquid Crystal Displays), memory chips and smart phone manufacturing. According to ITU, South Korea is also number one in ICT development (2011), and e-government readiness (2012).

South Korea is the most connected country in the world with its broadband connections and mobile network being the fastest in the world.

Smartphone users are expected to exceed 30 million by December 2012.

The South Korean Government continues to stimulate exporting and attract foreign companies. The government is fostering economies identified as the new growth engines in 'Green technology', 'High-tech convergence' and 'Value added service'

Key opportunities

1. Green Technology

This covers renewable energy and related technologies, low-carbon energy technology, green transportation systems and LEDs. The government has strongly led smart grid initiatives from 2009 and developed them into an intelligent power grid project. Foreign companies in technology driven energy areas will find opportunities in R&D collaboration with strong support from the South Korean government.

2. Big Data

With Jeju test beds running for almost two years, the consortium leaders start to see the importance of the massive data they have gathered. To transform all the different kinds of data into meaningful information to value add imperative business decisions, the South Korean companies look for data analysis expertise. Foreign companies in this area would find great opportunities in talking to many smart grid companies in South Korea.

3. Broadcasting Communications Media

With the 'digital switch over' project, all analogue broadcasting systems will be digitalised by the end of 2012. Accordingly, demand for broadcast-communications convergence technology, services and content will be high. Foreign companies with expertise in developing the next generation of convergence networks, wireless communication and security, 3D and multiple platforms technology for digital (smart) TV will find massive opportunities.

4. Content and Games

The content industry has grown by 14.6% in 2011 with 28.9% growth in export. Music and games are the top two industries that contributed to this movement. With more than 60% of the population using smart phones, mobile banking and other mobile commerce are big in the market. Foreign companies in mobile advertising, cloud technology and mobile security software companies would find opportunities in working with domestic companies. Similarly, transforming cultural content into digital format and developing related software will keep interest from the local companies.

5. Online and Mobile Games

In 2011 the games market was valued at approximately US$8 billion. Not only historically strong, massively multiplayer online role-playing games (MMORPG), but also smart phone games played a significant role in the growth. 2012 is expected to grow by 16% to more than US$9 billion. Serious games developers will find multiple opportunities with Korean partners in the healthcare, education, military and education sectors.

Finally the right approach to entering the South Korean market would be through collaboration. Rather than exporting goods to the South Korean market, finding local partners to tackle the markets together would be more probable in this complicated sector.

Foreign companies are recommended to have a capable local distributor, licensee or franchise partner who has an established network in the market and extensive market knowledge. A long-term perspective and a reliable partnership between supplier and their local partner is one of the key factors in achieving success.

Chapter 26: Food and Drink Sector in South Korea

South Korea is the 12th largest economy in the world and a G20 member state. The population of South Korea is 50 million and a predicted GDP growth of 3.8 percent in 2013, according to the Bank of Korea. The size of the food and drinks market in South Korea was estimated to be £74 billion and is expected to increase year on year by approximately 9 percent.

South Korea is currently dependent on imports for 60-70 percent of its food. This figure has been increasing in recent years as local agriculture and food production fails to keep pace with the increasing demand. Consumers are demanding healthy and convenient products, a trend that is consistent with consumer practices in affluent countries around the world.

Rapid economic growth and increasing income per capita has led to substantial changes in eating habits. Consumption of the main staple food, rice, has declined, while consumption of meat, fruit, vegetables and dairy products has increased. The younger generation's exposure to western-style foods, brands and tastes, through overseas travel and study, is increasing their familiarity and acceptance of Western food products.

The organic food market has been continuously growing over the last five years and is expected to

141

maintain this upward trend by 25-30 per cent. The organic food market has exceeded 4 trillion Korean Won in 2011.

Key opportunities

1. Alcoholic drinks

South Korea already is a huge importer of UK whisky. Where previously old blended whisky has been most popular, premium products and single malts are now gaining popularity in South Korea. South Korean consumers also consume light beers and lagers. Recently, imported premium lager, has been experiencing strong sales growth. The demand for beer amongst younger people as well as female drinkers is very high.

2. Coffee and Tea

The market for coffee is growing as South Koreans embrace the Western coffee culture. Although the American style is leading the coffee market, trendy consumers are increasingly looking to embrace the European style as well. In addition, tea still remains popular for its health benefits.

3. Ready Meals

Increasing numbers of dual-income families and single-parent households dominate the growth in pre-packaged ready meals. Plus, exposure of South Korea's younger generation to western-style foods, brands, and tastes through overseas travel and study is increasing their desire for ready meals. The FTA will affect the high duties currently in place on these products.

4. Cheese

Local prices for dairy products are high by global standards, and local producers only create a small amount of processed cheese. South Korean food processors are seeking reliable sources of high-quality and cost-competitive dairy ingredients. There are strong opportunities for foreign companies to supply dairy products and cheese particularly cheddar, as Stilton is considered too strong for South Korean tastes.

5. Meat and Fisheries

The farm products sector will benefit considerably from the FTA, especially those dealing in frozen pork, which is in high demand. Frozen pork belly accounts for up to 70 percent of pork imports and no quantity limitations are in place offering a good opportunity for EU suppliers. In addition, there are opportunities for the whelk meat and pollack

To compete in South Korea, foreign companies are recommended to have a capable, established and knowledgeable local distributor, licensee or franchise partner. A long-term perspective and a reliable partnership between supplier and their local partner is one of the key factors in achieving success.

Chapter 27: Environment Sector in South Korea

The South Korean government is investing heavily in new "low carbon, green growth" industries. It will invest £26 billion by 2013 on environmental projects in a "Green New Deal" to aid economic growth and create nearly a million jobs.

The projects cover the following areas: energy conservation, recycling and carbon reduction. This is in addition to flood prevention and development around the country's four main rivers and maintaining forest.

Key opportunities

South Korea is looking for technical and commercial cooperation to achieve its environmental targets.

1. Waste Management and Recycling

In 2009, the amount of waste generated per day was over 357,896 tonnes which was a decrease of 0.4 per cent on the previous year. The makeup of waste generated is municipal waste 14.2 per cent; industrial waste 34.5 per cent; and construction waste 51.2 per cent.

South Korea will invest USD$1.13 billion to expand recycling facilities, develop recycling technology and foster the recycling industry. The Korean

Government aims to reduce municipal waste by 12 per cent and landfill by 22 per cent by 2013. South Korea also wants to increase recycling by 53 per cent over the same time period.

2. Creating Energy from Waste (Landfill Gas)

Electricity and thermal energy generated from landfill sites is an area of priority for the Korean Government. Although projects like the Sudokwon (Metropolitan) Landfill Site have already started to utilise the carbon dioxide and methane gas produced inside landfills, the Ministry of Environment (MOE) plans to invest a total of US$3.2 billion between 2008 and 2013 to develop projects creating energy from waste.

3. Water Supply and Sewage

To meet the public need for high quality tap water, the MOE has initiated projects which will foster global competitiveness in the water industry through the restructuring of the tap water industry.

The size of the water industry is expected to grow to US$2 billion by 2015. To facilitate this MOE has set up a five year plan for fostering the water industry which started in 2007. This Governmental stimulus is seen as a key sector of growth in South Korea and consequently offers foreign companies great commercial potential.

4. Contaminated Land Remediation

In South Korea, there are five main causes of soil pollution: landfills; underground storage tanks; abandoned or inactive mines; disused military camps and industrial sites. The MOE established 250 stations nationwide in 1987 constituting the 'national soil monitoring network' and started routine monitoring. In 2006, it carried out a soil contamination investigation at over 2,200 sites with 1,500 stations and the MOE plans to increase this to 3,000 stations by 2015.

Chapter 28: Financial Sector in South Korea

South Korea has a highly developed and profitable financial services sector including the second largest insurance market and third largest banking market in Asia.

According to a recent data, Korea's competitiveness as a global financial centre has improved dramatically to become the 11th competitive centre in the world. Investment from international financial services groups is increasing, reflecting the economic potential and strengthening balance sheets of Korea's financial institutions.

The stability of the banking sector is underpinned by strong fundamentals and active regulation. At less than 1%, South Korea's non-performing loan ratio is low by regional standards. Foreign investors own some 70% of banking sector.

The asset management sector is set for rapid growth as a result of pension reform. More than a third of the country's 52 asset managers are now solely or jointly run by international groups.

Insurance remains dominated by a small number of local players. However, foreign companies have made strong inroads. Foreign entry in to the market has included both acquisition of existing companies and

Greenfield start-ups. Current flotation could open up new investment targets.

The relaxation of controls on cross-ownership of financial services will further open up opportunities for market entry, acquisition and business development. As international financial services groups look to develop their footprint in Asia, a presence in South Korea is becoming desirable, if not essential.

Key opportunities

Financial Investment Services and Capital Market Act (FSCMA)

The FSCMA came into force in February 2009. The new law was meant to reshape the landscape of the industry by breaking down regulatory barriers separating stock brokerages, futures trading and asset management, thus encouraging market consolidation to form large, internationally competitive players.

The Act is comparable to the UK's 'Big Bang' or the repeal of the Glass-Steagall Act in the US. A key aim is to enable larger securities companies to provide a broader and more sophisticated range of capital market products and fee-generating services. The Act also encourages greater cross-selling and cross-ownership within the sector. The Act has been recently revised to aim at introducing home-grown hedge funds to Korea's capital markets.

1. Banking

Hana Financial Group's acquisition of Korea Exchange Bank will turn the former into a major force in the domestic market, but a fiercer competition within the sector could put a ceiling on South Korean banks' profitability. Following Hana's expansionary move, there will be four strong banking groups (Shinhan, KB Kookmin, Woori & Hana) with similar asset sizes, suggesting that the highly-saturated sector could see competition intensify further.

Long-term strategic investors have moved into the market in recent years, in many cases acquiring the stakes of an earlier wave of private equity buyers. The FSCMA could open up new opportunities for cross-selling to bank customers, including further development of Bank assurance and capital market business.

2. Asset management

The market size is still small compared with the size of other developed economies. The value of managed assets was US$274.8 billion as of end of September 2011, ranking 15th among 46 countries.

The asset management sector is set for rapid growth as a result of pension reform. South Korea's retirement pension fund has been growing at more than 100% per year, while the private pension fund has been expanding at an average of 15% per year.

3. Insurance

Foreign entry into the market has included both company acquisition and greenfield start-ups. Recent listings of life insurers may create new investment targets. Despite the global economic slowdown, annual insurance premium maintained a high growth trend in 2011 due to changes in the financial environment as well as diversifying consumer needs. The on-going demand for after-retirement protection-type products as well as health insurance products, including accident and illness, and medical expense coverage products are expected to drive this growth. In life insurance sector, sales of both annuities and savings insurance products are in high demand among consumers. Non-life insurance premiums growth was mainly driven by growing demand for long term insurance and automobile insurance. Samsung Life, Korea Life and Kyobo Life dominate the South Korean life insurance market, accounting for more than half of all life-insurance premiums whereas Samsung Fire and Marine is the largest non-life insurer.

Moreover, adoption of IFRS (International Financial Reporting Standards) in 2011 and introduction of risk based capital system (RBC) has contributed to strengthen risk management and improve financial prudence of insurers. It is expected that South Korean insurance sector will grow in coming years on account of more demand for retirement pension scheme, health insurance policies and introduction of new products/policies with more benefits as well as protection.

4. Sovereign Wealth Funds/Pension Funds

Particular opportunities for asset management and property management companies are to work alongside the likes of the National Pension Service ('NPS'). Their fund is the fourth largest pension fund in the world with assets of $300 billion. They will have to outsource their increasing assets to more financial service companies, pushing up the demand for funds. They are already working with some UK asset and real estate management companies and purchased three iconic buildings in London in 2009 including HSBC HQ in Canary Wharf and 88 Wood Street in the City of London.

The Korea Investment Corporation: a sovereign wealth fund has shown an interest in real estate and other alternative products in UK. They opened an office in London on 1 December 2011 and recently acquired an office building in the City of London.

Other pension funds such as the Teachers' Pension Fund and the Korea Post are also interested in working with UK companies.

To compete in South Korea UK companies are recommended to have a capable local partner who has an established network in the market and extensive market knowledge.

A long-term perspective and a reliable partnership between supplier and their local partner is one of the key factors in achieving success.

Chapter 29: Conclusion

In a highly competitive business environment, it is more important than ever to understand the business culture of your target markets. Understanding business culture helps you to understand, anticipate and respond to unexpected behaviour. It also ensures that you behave in an acceptable way and avoid misunderstandings.

South Korea split from North Korea in 1948, the North becoming a communist dictatorship allied with the, then, USSR and the South allying with the US to become a leading industrial nation. In 1950, South Korea was invaded by North Korea.

The ensuing Korean War ended in 1953 without a peace agreement. Over a period of four decades, South Korea transformed itself into one of the world's major economies. After years of authoritarian rule, a multi-party political system was introduced in 1987.

Relations with North Korea remain a concern, particularly in view of the North's nuclear ambitions. Until 2008, South Korea pursued a "sunshine" policy of engagement with its neighbour, refusing international calls for sanctions over the North's nuclear programme. However, President Lee Myung-bak, elected in 2008, has adopted a tougher tone against the North.

Tensions rose in 2009 when the North conducted a series of missile tests. Relations worsened further in 2010 following a cross-border clash. The demilitarised zone between North and South Korea remains one of the world's most heavily fortified frontiers.

According to government statistics, nearly half (46 per cent) of all South Koreans claim to have no particular religious beliefs. The main religion in South Korea is Christianity (29.2 per cent), followed by Buddhism (22.8 per cent). Both main religions have been widely influenced by Korean Confucianism.

Corruption remains an issue in South Korea. In 2010, the country was ranked 39th on Transparency International's corruption perception index. This is up from 40th place in 2008 and 43rd in 2007, so the country is moving in the right direction. Nevertheless, as the 12th-largest economy in the world, one might expect South Korea's business economy to be more transparent than it is. Although the number of cases of corruption in the public arena has decreased, the authorities have yet to stamp out bribery and corruption completely.

South Korea has its own language (Korean) and alphabet (Hangul). Hangul consists of 10 vowels and 14 basic consonants. You will find a basic explanation of Korean vowels and consonants on the Korea.net website.

Korean is the official business language of South Korea. However, English is widely spoken amongst senior business people and government officials.

While high-level business meetings may be conducted mainly in English, your hosts will appreciate it if you use their language whenever possible. When speaking in English, remember to talk slowly and repeat key points. In order to save face, your Korean hosts will not necessarily say that they don't understand something.

Interpreters may be required for business meetings, particularly outside Seoul and other major cities. All important negotiations should be carried out with an interpreter present so as to avoid doubt. It is also advisable to have all written documents translated into Korean.

Some common phrases
1. Good morning: An nyeong ha se yo
2. Good afternoon: An nyeong ha se yo
3. Good evening: An nyeong ha se yo
4. Good night: An nyong hi ju mu se yo
5. Goodbye: An nyeong hi ga se yo
6. See you again: To man na yo
7. Yes: Ne
8. No: Ah Ni Yo
9. Please: Bu tak ham ni da
10. Thank you: Gam Sa Ham Ni Da
11. Please sit down: An Jeu Se Yo
12. Please come in: Tu ro ose yo
13. Excuse me: Sil ley ham ni da
14. I come from: Eso wat seub ni da
15. My name is: Je ireum eun
16. What is your name? Ireum i mu eot ip ni ka?
17. Can you speak English? Young eo ha se yo?

Good luck!

www.ingramcontent.com/pod-product-compliance
Lightning Source LLC
Chambersburg PA
CBHW051703170526
45167CB00002B/515